Praise for
THE PROBLEM WITH SOCIALISM

"Like in a bad horror movie, once-dead socialism has come back to life in the United States, capturing the attention of many young people with promises of free things. Our public education system fails miserably in teaching students about the millions of graves filled over the past century by the horrors of socialism. Fortunately, we still have writers like Professor Thomas DiLorenzo to shine light on the socialist lie and guide the youth to the real guarantor of happiness and prosperity: a free society. DiLorenzo's book is a pleasure to read and should be put in the hands of every young person in this country—and elsewhere!"

—Former Congressman Ron Paul

"With so many universities having been turned into socialist indoctrination academies, it is a worthwhile investment for parents with college-age children to buy two copies of *The Problem With Socialism*—one for their children and one for themselves."

—Walter E. Williams, John M. Olin Distinguished Professor of Economics, George Mason University and nationally syndicated columnist

"Utterly faithful to the first principles of von Mises and Hayek, and consistent with his myth-busting works on Lincoln and Hamilton, Professor Thomas DiLorenzo has given us another fearless masterpiece. In *The Problem With Socialism*, he skillfully dissects the intellectual bankruptcy and false reality that have been the earmarks of the systemic legalized theft that socialism became wherever it was tried. We already know that rather than freedom, prosperity, and hope, socialism brought chains, misery, and despair. Now we have that history clearly documented in this powerful, unassailable, and readable book which should be mandatory reading wherever Economics 101 is taught."

—Hon. Andrew P. Napolitano, Senior Judicial Analyst, Fox News Channel, and Distinguished Visiting Professor of Law, Brooklyn Law School

"Ever wonder what *one book* you should give a young person to make sure he doesn't fall for leftist propaganda? You're looking at it. Tom DiLorenzo smashes socialism in theory and in practice, and in all its poverty-inducing forms. Guaranteed those college socialists don't know any of this material—at most American universities, who on earth would have taught it to them? Dance on socialism's grave by reading this book."

—Thomas E. Woods Jr., host of *The Tom Woods Show*, and author of the *New York Times* bestseller *The Politically Incorrect Guide® to American History*

THE PROBLEM WITH SOCIALISM

THE PROBLEM WITH SOCIALISM

THOMAS DiLORENZO

REGNERY
PUBLISHING
A Division of Salem Media Group

Regnery® is a registered trademark of Salem Communications Holding Corporation

Cataloging-in-Publication Data on file with the Library of Congress

ISBN 978-1-62157-589-4

Published in the United States by
Regnery Publishing
A Division of Salem Media Group
300 New Jersey Ave NW
Washington, DC 20001
www.Regnery.com

Manufactured in the United States of America

10 9 8 7 6 5 4 3 2 1

Books are available in quantity for promotional or premium use. For information on discounts and terms, please visit our website: www.Regnery.com.

Distributed to the trade by
Perseus Distribution
250 West 57th Street
New York, NY 10107

Dedicated to all the victims of socialism—
past, present, and future

CONTENTS

As Margaret Thatcher famously said,
the problem with socialism and socialists is,
"They always run out of other people's money."

1

THE PROBLEM WITH SOCIALISM

A quarter of a century after the spectacular collapse of socialism in the Soviet empire, a large segment of the "millennial" generation of young Americans (those born between 1982 and 2004) thinks socialism may be the wave of *their* future. A 2015 "yougov.com" poll revealed that 43 percent of Americans between the ages of eighteen and twenty-nine had a "favorable" opinion of socialism and that they have a higher opinion of socialism than they do of capitalism.[1] (Who says the public schools are not teaching the kids much these days?)

A 2016 Pew Foundation poll found that 69 percent of voters under the age of thirty expressed "a willingness to vote for a socialist president of the United States"; and literally millions of millennials voted for self-described "democratic" socialist, Senator Bernie Sanders, in the Democratic Party primaries in 2016.[2] Sanders won majorities of the under-thirty vote in several major state primaries campaigning on a platform of "free" higher education, "free" healthcare, and a vastly increased welfare state.

Did America "forget what 'socialist' means," asked one pundit in response to this youthful fascination with neo-Marxism.[3] Apparently so. Just as apparent is the fact that many younger Americans believe that there *is* a Santa Claus after all (stripped of all his religious significance as Saint Nicholas, of course) who can—and should—give them "free" education, "free" healthcare, "free" whatever they want, because they deserve it. But government is not Santa Claus and nothing is free. Uncle Sam has not been replaced by Uncle Santa. *Someone* has to pay for all those doctors, nurses, hospitals, medicines, x-ray machines, ambulances, and everything else associated with healthcare. The public schools are not "free" either; they are paid for with billions of dollars in property taxes and other taxes imposed by federal, state, and local governments. The same goes for "free" higher education that is occasionally promised by political demagogues like Senator Sanders.

What socialists like Senator Sanders should say if they want to be truthful and straightforward is not that government can offer citizens anything for free, but that they want healthcare (and much else) to become a government-run monopoly financed entirely *with taxes.* Taxes *hide,* but do not eliminate, the cost of individual government programs. No one gets an itemized tax bill denoting how much goes for national defense, how much for the Department of Labor, how much for the Environmental Protection Agency, how much for celebrating Lesbian, Gay, Bisexual, and Transgender Pride Month (established by President Obama in June 2009), and all the rest. Consequently, it is indeed difficult to know exactly how much of one's taxes goes for any particular program. But nothing about government is ever free. According to the Tax Foundation, working Americans toil, on average, until the end of April each year—one-third of the year—just to pay all the taxes owed to federal, state, and local governments.[4] After that they can begin working for themselves and their families.

Does anyone really believe that turning *any* industry into a tax-financed, Department-of-Motor-Vehicles-style, government-run monopoly (which is what socialism is) will make things cheaper (or free) instead of substantially *more* expensive? History and all worldly experience would suggest that the latter is true, and that socialism (government-run monopolies for healthcare or anything else) *reduces* the quality of products and services offered to the public.

WHAT WE MUST FORGET

In order to have a "favorable" view of socialism one must have either forgotten what the entire world learned about socialism from the late nineteenth century on, or have never learned anything about it in the first place. The latter is obviously true of much of the younger generation.

Socialism started out being defined as "government ownership of the means of production," which is why the government of the Soviet Union confiscated all businesses, factories, and farms, murdering millions of dissenters and resisters in the process. It is also why socialist political parties in Europe, once in power, nationalized as many of the major industries (steel, automobiles, coal mines, electricity, telephone services) as they could. The Labour Party in post-World War II Great Britain would be an example of this. All of this was done, ostensibly, in the name of pursuing material "equality."

In the foreword to the 1976 edition of his famous book, *The Road to Serfdom*,[5] Nobel laureate economist

Friedrich Hayek wrote that the definition of "socialism" evolved in the twentieth century to mean income redistribution in pursuit of "equality," not through government ownership of the means of production but through the institutions of the welfare state and the "progressive" income tax. The means may have changed, but the ostensible end—equality—remained the same.

Hayek's mentor, fellow Austrian economist Ludwig von Mises, explained in his classic treatise *Socialism: An Economic and Sociological Analysis,*[6] that the welfare state, the "progressive" income tax, and especially pervasive government regulation of business were all tools of "destructionism" in the eyes of the socialists of his day. That is, he observed that the proponents of socialism always employed a two-pronged approach: (1) the government takeover of as many industries and as much land as possible, and (2) attempts to destroy existing capitalist societies with onerous taxes, regulations, the welfare state, inflation, or whatever they thought could get the job done.

We must forget (or be oblivious to) an awful lot of not-so-ancient history to have a "favorable" view of socialism. We must be unaware of how it is a form of economic poison that destroys prosperity and is the biggest generator of poverty the world has ever known. In the early twentieth century it turned Ukraine from "the breadbasket of Europe" to a desolate, barren land where the people could hardly feed themselves let alone export food to anyone else in just a few years. It had the same effect all throughout the world in countries that adopted socialized agriculture.

When the Chilean government adopted socialism in the early 1970s and nationalized industries and farms, the economy ground to a halt and the government did what all socialist governments eventually do to bail themselves out: it printed massive amounts of money to attempt to keep the economy—which it had all but destroyed—going. The result was that the cost of living rose by 746 percent (the annual inflation rate); unemployment was sky high; and the government was eventually replaced in a coup by a repressive regime.[7]

The Soviet economy was so dysfunctional, thanks to seventy years of socialism, that by the time the entire system collapsed in the late 1980s it was most probably only about 5 percent of the size of the U.S. economy according to Dr. Yuri Maltsev, an American economics professor who was an advisor to Mikhail Gorbachev, the last president of the Soviet Union. This was despite the Soviet Union's vast natural resources, unrivaled by any other country or political empire. Soviet socialism never produced a single product that succeeded in international competition, with the possible exception of Russian caviar which comes from a fish (the sturgeon), not a factory. All of the socialist "satellite" countries of the Soviet Union suffered a similar economic fate, from Romania, Czechoslovakia, and East Germany to Cuba and beyond. In socialist country after socialist country, the common people were equal in their poverty while the political elite lived privileged lives. The entire world celebrated the demise of Soviet socialism, but nowhere was the celebration as great as among the millions of surviving victims of socialism who lived under the boot of the Soviet empire.

Great Britain adopted its brand of "democratic" socialism, known as "Fabian socialism," after World War II as it nationalized many key industries, imposed very high rates of taxation, established a massive welfare state, and adopted socialized medicine and government-funded pensions. Britain had been the wealthiest country in the world up to the beginning of World War I, so it was able to live off of the "capital" created by previous generations of British entrepreneurs for a while. But within twenty years the entire world was talking about "the British disease," a phrase that was used to describe the gross inefficiency of all those socialist, government-run monopolies in the British steel, automobile, telephone, electric, and other industries.

By the 1970s the British had had enough. After thirty years of Fabian socialism, they elected Margaret Thatcher prime minister. A student of Friedrich Hayek and other free-market economists, she privatized many of Britain's nationalized industries. For decades, Great Britain had been falling behind other European democracies in terms of per-capita income. That trend was reversed by Thatcher's desocialization programs.[8]

Another example of an economic catastrophe caused by the adoption of "democratic" socialism is the country of Argentina, which embraced socialism in the late 1940s during the Juan Perón regime. Perón restricted international trade, imposed wage-and-price controls, seized private property, nationalized some industries, and spent lavishly, much of which was financed by the government simply printing more money. The predictable result was economic ruination and hyperinflation that led to Perón's ouster in 1955 by military coup. Argentina, however, remained socialist. Its economy continued to stagnate and, several coups later, by the late 1980s, it was suffering from 12,000 percent inflation from years of trying to cover up the failures of socialism by printing money to pay for all the socialist programs.[9]

In 2001 Argentina defaulted on its obligations to foreign lenders in the then-largest public default in history. It defaulted again in 2014. Argentina was once the world's tenth-largest economy, but by 2016 it was barely ahead of Kazakhstan and Equatorial Guinea.[10]

India was once one of the wealthiest countries on earth. Its textile industry was the envy of the world; it had sophisticated financial markets, many talented entrepreneurs, millions of acres of fertile farmland, and plenty of extravagant wealth. When it gained independence from Britain in 1947, it was no longer one of the richest nations on earth, but it inherited an infrastructure of railroads and schools and ports and parliamentary institutions and law, and the lingua franca of English. Unfortunately, in rebellion against the traditions of its "capitalist-imperialist" masters (but in accord with intellectual fashion), it adopted a home-grown version of Soviet-style central economic planning. Under Prime Minister Nehru and his top economic planning minister, Prasanta Chandra Mahalanobis, India adopted a series of "Five-Year Plans" modeled after the notoriously failed Soviet Five-Year Plans. The Marxist economic model that was used to justify these "plans" was one that was first developed by a Soviet economist named G.A. Feldman. It eventually came to be known as the "Feldman-Mahalanobis model" for a socialist, centrally planned economy.[11] It was no more successful in India than it was in the Soviet Union as India, after independence, became synonymous with "poverty." In the 1980s, Indian Prime Minister Rajiv Gandhi essentially gave up on socialism and cut taxes and deregulated and privatized industries. The result was that India's economy finally became revitalized and started to create wider prosperity.

Economist George Ayittey, a professor at American University and native of Ghana, is the author of several scholarly books about how socialism destroyed the economies of many post-colonial African countries that rejected capitalism and adopted socialism in the 1960s.[12] African leaders took the position that "Soviet-style socialism with the state determining the economic destiny of the people" was the best way "to move Africa toward economic prosperity."[13] "Many foreign companies were nationalized, and numerous state-owned enterprises were established. Roadblocks and passbook systems were employed to control the movement of Africans. Marketing boards and export regulations were tightened to fleece the cash crop producers. Price controls were imposed on farmers and merchants. Bewildering arrays of restrictions were imposed on imports, capital transfers, industry, wages, trade unions, prices, rents, interest rates, and the like."[14] "Only socialism will save Africa" was the slogan of African political elites.[15] The result was that, forty years later, these African countries were *poorer* than they had been as colonies. The African political elites, however, were fabulously wealthy, with billions of dollars stolen from public treasuries and bribery a necessary condition to get anything done.

Socialism is "as alien to Africa as it is to the rest of the world," wrote Professor Ayittey, who recounts the long history of private property and entrepreneurship among Africans before the "alien ideology" of socialism was imposed after independence. "[N]obody can defend socialism on the basis of the African tradition," he concluded.[16]

For most of the Cold War years the starkest difference between a capitalist and a socialist economy was the comparison of Communist China with nearby Hong Kong. Hong Kong was one of the freest economies in the world under British rule with a modest, flat income tax and very little government regulation of business. That recipe made Hong Kong, with no natural resources to speak of except for a large harbor, one of the most prosperous countries on earth. By contrast, socialist China experienced the usual economic stagnation and backwardness that is the hallmark of all socialist economies.

China abruptly liberalized a large part of its economy beginning in the late 1970s by allowing private enterprises and even private banks, to some extent, to exist. The creation of a free enterprise segment of the Chinese economy, combined with the typical Chinese/Confucian work ethic and entrepreneurial spirit that is on display all over the world, began to produce prosperity. By the beginning of the twenty-first century China had become one of the biggest, if not *the* biggest, manufacturing economies in the world. A little bit of desocialization can go a very long way in terms of creating prosperity and eliminating poverty in previously socialist countries. China has a long way to go, but its people have benefited greatly from these first steps away from socialism.

What also must be forgotten if one is to have a "favorable" opinion of socialism is that government control of an economy, whether done in the name of "equality," environmentalism, or anything else, has long been associated with the destruction of civil liberties, especially freedom of speech. Government planners throughout the world are intolerant of public criticisms of their grandiose plans. In some socialist countries like the former Soviet Union criticizing the government led to imprisonment—or worse. In less totalitarian socialist states, criticisms are censored or outlawed. As one student of socialist societies put it, a key trait of socialism is "a profound opposition to personal liberty and scorn for individual reason, a complete contempt for the individual. They unceasingly attempt to mutilate, to curtail, to obstruct personal freedom in any and all ways."[17]

This book will serve as a primer on socialism (and capitalism) for some; a historical reminder for others; and a handy sourcebook on all the problems of socialism and how it threatens a free society. Along the way, we will examine how egalitarianism is at war with human nature; why so many of "the worst" people have risen to power under socialism; why fascism is just another form of socialism; how the "success" of Scandinavian socialism is a myth; how the welfare state and the "progressive" income tax actually exacerbate inequality; why pollution and other environmental problems are far *worse* under socialism; why minimum-wage laws, government-run school monopolies, and socialized financial markets fail; and why more socialism inevitably means less freedom. What follows is the truth about socialism—and what it will mean if it becomes our future.

2

WHY SOCIALISM IS ALWAYS AND EVERYWHERE AN ECONOMIC DISASTER

Socialism in all its forms has always been poisonous to economic growth and prosperity. This is not because the "wrong people" have been in charge of socialist regimes, and that "better" or smarter people could somehow make socialism work, or that all that is missing is democracy. Socialism is economic poison for several fundamental, inherent reasons. In other words, it is impossible for socialism to be anything but impoverishing as an economic system because of the very nature of socialism.

Every imaginable type of socialism was tried in the nineteenth and twentieth centuries, producing nothing but economic stagnation—or much worse. Some post-colonial African countries, like Zimbabwe, went from being economic breadbaskets to economic hell-holes.[1] But everywhere, from Britain, India, and Latin America to Africa, socialism brought economic ruin. Worse, in the Soviet Union, China, North Korea, and Cambodia, it manufactured not just poverty, but mass executions numbering in the millions and the most tyrannical regimes in human history.

At a minimum, socialism has what economists would categorize as an "incentive problem"; a "knowledge problem"; and an "economic calculation problem." A good example of the incentive problem involves the first American pilgrims.

HOW SOCIALISM ALMOST DESTROYED AMERICA

The first American settlers originally adopted communal or socialized ownership of land and property. As a result, most of them rather quickly starved to death or died of disease.

When the first pilgrims arrived in Jamestown, Virginia, in May 1607 they found incredibly fertile soil and plentiful seafood, wild game, and fruits of all kinds. Despite all of this, within six months all but thirty-eight of the original 104 Jamestown settlers were dead, having starved.[2] Two years later, 500 more pilgrims arrived in Virginia, transported there by the Virginia Company, and a shocking 440 of them died from starvation or disease. This became known as "the starving time," described by one eye witness: "So great was our famine, that a savage we slew and buried, the poorer sorte took him up againe and eat him; and so did divers one another boyled and stewed with roots and herbs."[3] This man also remarked that the cause of the starvation was "want of providence" and "industrie" and "not the barenness and defect of the Countrie, as is generally supposed."[4] In other words, the problem was lack of effort, not a lack of resources.

The essential problem was that all of the pilgrims were indentured servants who had no financial stake in the fruits of their own labor. All that they produced went into a common pool to be used to generate profits for the Virginia Company as compensation for transporting them to America, and to support the colony. Working harder, longer, or smarter produced no additional benefit to anyone because the system that was set up was essentially agricultural socialism and everyone was compensated the same regardless of individual effort. The absence of property rights in the land, and of any link between effort and reward, destroyed the work ethic of the pilgrims, just as it always does in any socialist society, whether that of the Jamestown pilgrims or that of the former Soviet Union.

Historian Philip A. Bruce wrote of the Jamestown pilgrims that the men idled over their tasks or refused to work altogether, and men who were known to be young and energetic by nature were "derelict."[5]

In 1611 the British government sent Sir Thomas Dale to serve as the "high marshal" of the Virginia colony. Dale noted that the surviving settlers were healthy and spent much of their time playing games and other vigorous activities. He immediately identified the source of the colony's problem as the system of socialized land ownership. Consequently, he determined that each man would be given three acres of private land from which he was only required to pay a tax of two-and-a-half barrels of corn to the Virginia Company. Everything else was his to keep or sell.

The Jamestown pilgrims then began to prosper. Each man realized that by loafing or shirking, he was paying the full cost of such behavior in the form of lost profits. At the same time, everyone realized that *increased* effort led to increased rewards. As historian Matthew Page Andrews wrote, "As soon as the settlers were thrown upon their own resources, and each freeman had acquired the right of owning property, the colonists quickly developed what became the distinguishing characteristic of Americans—an aptitude for all kinds of craftsmanship coupled with an innate genius for experimentation and invention."[6]

The private property system that replaced agricultural socialism in the Jamestown colony was quickly expanded so that each settler who paid his own way was given fifty acres of land, and by 1623 all land had been converted to private ownership. Capitalism replaced socialism and the pilgrims thrived.

The same tragic mistake of adopting agricultural socialism was made in the Massachusetts colony where about half of the original pilgrims who landed in Cape Cod in 1620 were dead within a few months. Fortunately, the leader of the Mayflower expedition, William Bradford, recognized the problem:

> For the young men that were most able and fit for labour and service, did repine that they should spend their time and strength to work for other men's wives and children without any recompense. The strong, or man of parts, had no more division of victuals and clothes than he that was weak and not able to do a quarter the other could; this was thought injustice.... And for men's wives to be commanded to do service for other men, as dressing their meat, washing their clothes, etc., they deemed it a kind of slavery, neither could many husbands brook it.[7]

Socialism was the root cause of the starving pilgrims in the original Massachusetts colony. Bradford recognized this and, like his Virginia predecessors, decided to abandon agricultural socialism and allow private property ownership. In his own words, it was decided that the pilgrims of Massachusetts

> ...should set corn for every man for his own particular, and in that regard trust to themselves; in all other things to go on in the general way as before. And so assigned to every family a parcel of land, for present use...and ranged all boys and youth under some family. This had very good success, for it made all hands very industrious, so as much more corn was planted.... The women now went willingly into the field, and took their little ones with them to set corn; which before would allege weakness and inability....[8]

By 1650 privately owned farms were as predominant in Massachusetts as they were in Virginia and elsewhere in the colonies, and the American economy began to thrive and prosper. The institutions of private property and free markets led to a burst of entrepreneurship and wealth creation. By 1776 the young

American economy was a hundred times larger than it was in the 1630s, and Americans had already become among the most affluent people in the world.[9]

As has been proven hundreds of times in world history, whenever socialism is applied, economic disaster, even to the point of starvation, follows. As the economist Murray Rothbard wrote, by the early twentieth century:

> [E]veryone, socialists and non-socialists alike, had long realized that socialism suffered from an incentive problem. If, for example, everyone under socialism were to receive an equal income, or, in another variant, everyone was supposed to produce 'according to his ability' but receive 'according to his needs,' then, to sum it up in the famous question: Who, under socialism, will take out the garbage? That is, what will be the incentive to do the grubby jobs, and, furthermore, to do them well? Or, to put it another way, what would be the incentive to work hard and be productive at *any* job?[10]

One hundred and fifty years of experiments with socialism in dozens of countries, large and small, proved the truthfulness of Rothbard's admonition. Russia was the world's largest exporter of grain before adopting socialism in 1917. Because of socialized agriculture, as many as ten million Russians died of starvation in the 1920s and 1930s. When Mao Tse Tung socialized Chinese agriculture, as many as thirty million Chinese starved to death between 1959 and 1962. Socialism produced horrifying human disasters in Cambodia, Ghana, Ethiopia, Tanzania, and other countries during the twentieth century.[11]

The exact same kinds of results occurred in manufacturing and all other industries under twentieth-century socialism. For as economist David Osterfeld wrote: "[S]ocialism, *by its very nature*, rewards sloth and indolence and penalizes diligence and hard work. It therefore establishes incentives that are incompatible with its self-proclaimed goal of material prosperity. The inherent dilemma of socialism is that individuals who respond 'rationally' to the incentives confronting them will produce results that are 'irrational' for the community as a whole."[12]

In the early twentieth century some socialists argued that socialism would somehow rather magically transform human beings, effectively taking the place of God to create a new "socialist man" who would no longer be acquisitive and interested in pursuing his own self-interest. This was long ago proven to be a farce, as it never occurred anywhere on earth despite the use of terror and mass murder by the former Soviet Union, China, Cuba, and other socialist regimes in vain attempts to "prove" their theory to be correct.[13]

THE KNOWLEDGE PROBLEM

A second reason for the inherent and inescapable failures of socialism as an economic system is known in the economics profession as the "knowledge problem." This problem is associated with the writings of the Nobel prize-winning economist Friedrich Hayek, who first explained the idea in a 1945 academic journal article entitled "The Use of Knowledge in Society."[14] In that article Hayek explained that the kind of knowledge that makes the economic world go 'round is not just scientific knowledge but the detailed and idiosyncratic "knowledge of the particular circumstances of time and place" that the millions of people who make up the world economy possess and utilize to perform their unique jobs and live their lives. No government planner could possibly possess, let alone efficiently utilize, such vast knowledge.

For example, consider something as simple as a slice of pizza. What would it take to make a pizza from scratch? Well, the first ingredient would be dough, which would require a wheat farm to raise the wheat that is turned into flour, which in turn is turned into pizza dough. The wheat farm requires all of the engineering know-how that is used to build all of the tractors and other farm equipment; farm tools, fertilizers, irrigation systems, and what not. Then there is the grain storage business and all that goes into it, along with the trucking industry that is used to transport the grain. The transportation industry requires gasoline or diesel fuel, which means the petroleum industry must become involved, including all of the sophisticated engineering knowledge that is used to extract petroleum from the earth (or the ocean floor) and refine it into gasoline.

So far, considering just one ingredient of a common pizza—dough—we learn that it requires the efforts of probably hundreds if not thousands of people from all over the world, all with very specialized "knowledge of the particular circumstances of time and place" that they use to do their jobs.

Then there is the tomato sauce, which requires a tomato farm and all the farm equipment, tools, fertilizers, irrigation, transportation, and so forth that is involved in growing and marketing tomatoes. A dairy farm is then needed to produce milk, which is turned into cheese for the pizza. And on and on. The lesson here is that what makes the economic world—indeed, human civilization itself as we know it—possible is the international division of labor *and knowledge* in which we all specialize in something in the marketplace, earn money doing it, and use that money to buy things from other "specialists." All of this occurs spontaneously without any government "planner" consciously dictating how to make pizzas, how many to make, or where pizza parlors should be located.

As Adam Smith explained in his famous 1776 treatise, *An Inquiry into the Nature and Causes of the Wealth of Nations*, what motivates people to put forth all of this effort and cooperate with each other to give us "our meat and our bread" is not their selflessness or their love of their fellow man, but their concern for their own wellbeing. By pursuing their own self-interest in the free market, they coincidentally, as though led by an "invisible hand," benefit the rest of society as well. As for socialism, it is worth repeating that no government planner or group of government planners with the most powerful computers available could conceivably possess and utilize all of the *constantly changing* information that is needed to produce even the most common and simple consumer goods, let alone sophisticated products like automobiles and computers.

The false notion that government planners under socialism could possess and make better use of all this information than the myriad consumers, workers, entrepreneurs, business managers, and other market participants in thousands of different industries was labeled "the pretense of knowledge" by Hayek in his Nobel prize acceptance speech in 1975. It was, said Hayek, the "fatal conceit" of socialists everywhere.

Hayek also pointed out how the free-market pricing system is indispensable as a tool of any functioning economy. Government-mandated prices, such as we have in socialist economies, produce nothing but chaos. In a market economy, prices are like road signs; in this case, they reflect the relative scarcity of goods and services, the intensity of consumer demand, and help us order our economic lives. When a product or service becomes more scarce consumers look for alternatives, which is one engine of innovation. When prices rise, investors are alerted to consumer demand and look to provide consumers with what they want at a lower price or to improve on the existing product or service.

Without market prices, rational economic decision making is impossible, which is another core reason for the failures of socialism to produce anything but poverty, misery, and economic chaos.

THE CALCULATION PROBLEM

The most devastating critique of socialism is known as the "calculation problem." Economist Ludwig von

Mises explained it in his 1920 treatise, *Socialism: An Economic and Sociological Analysis*,[15] and in his later 1949 treatise, *Human Action*.[16] Socialists who advocate government "planning" with government ownership of the means of production face an impossible task, said Mises, because they have no idea how to go about arranging the production of goods and services without real, market-based capital markets (such as the stock market, private banking system, and so on). It is capitalist entrepreneurs, Mises wrote, the professional speculators, promoters, investors, and lenders, who all have a *personal financial stake* in the investments they make, who allocate capital in a *market* economy. Their indispensable tool is market prices, which guide them to invest in a rational, profitable way, meeting consumer demand. Under socialism, where government owns all the means of production and capital "markets" are nonexistent, and resources are allocated by bureaucrats to meet "plans" that might have no basis in economic reality.

In a capitalist economy, entrepreneurs have to meet consumer demand or go bankrupt. This doesn't mean that capitalist markets are "perfect," only that there is an enormously powerful incentive for private investors to invest their money in ways that will be rewarded by consumers. This incentive, however, is totally absent from a socialist economy, where it is not consumer demand (and the investors' desire to make a profit and avoid a loss), but government direction, that allocates economic resources, which is why Mises deemed socialism to be "impossible" as a viable economic system; it simply makes no economic sense.

Some seventy years after Ludwig von Mises first explained the impossibility of rational economic calculation under socialism, the well-known socialist economist Robert Heilbroner authored a momentous essay in *The New Yorker* entitled "The Triumph of Capitalism," in which he begrudgingly admitted that "Mises was right" about socialism all along.[17] At the time, the seventy-year-old Heilbroner was the Norman Thomas Professor of Economics at the New School for Social Research and had spent the previous thirty years of his academic career advocating and defending socialism. (Norman Thomas was a twentieth-century presidential candidate of the American Socialist Party.)

The point here is to note the irony of the renewed popularity of "socialism" today, especially among a segment of the college student population, when even longtime twentieth-century defenders of socialism such as Robert Heilbroner finally admitted that it was a massively failed and misconceived idea. To be a modern-day advocate of socialism is to completely ignore all sound economic logic, more than a century of history, and the words of honest socialist intellectuals like

Heilbroner who were finally forced to confront reality after ignoring it for most of their adult lives.

3

EGALITARIANISM VERSUS HUMAN REALITY

The pervasive rallying cry of socialists is "equality." Capitalism creates too many inequities, they say. But they ignore the fact that all human beings are unique, and inequality is thus inevitable.

The relentless socialist crusade for "equality" is not just a revolt against reality; it is nothing less than a recipe for the destruction of normal human society, as the Russian and Chinese socialists of the twentieth century, among others, proved. In the name of socialist equality they destroyed their economies, condemned hundreds of millions to poverty, and executed millions of dissenters.[1] And even after all that, they never created anything remotely like an egalitarian society.

Democratic-socialist countries that have not gone to these murderous extremes have nevertheless been content to live off of the capital accumulated from limited or previous free markets in their countries.

Socialists are less concerned about equality before the law, or equal rights to liberty, than they are with *material* equality, which, of necessity, has to be forced upon society by the state. Rabbi Daniel Lapin, a clergyman who is also an economic writer and speaker,[2] points out that anything made by God, whether it be humans or stones (which can range from small pebbles to glittering diamonds of infinite variety) is unique; while things made by man, like bricks, can be made uniform. The essence of the socialist enterprise is to use the coercive powers of government to turn us all into identical bricks.

The desire to turn unique human beings into identical socialist bricks explains why socialist regimes are often totalitarian—because it is the only way they can make a serious attempt to achieve their aims.

The socialist obsession with equality has always been at war with the division of labor and knowledge that comes naturally in a market or capitalist economy. Ludwig von Mises noted that "The fundamental social phenomenon is the division of labor and its counterpart, human cooperation,"[3] which, in turn, is what leads to economic progress and development.

The uniqueness of every human being—our differing physical abilities, mental abilities and interests, different aptitudes, preferences *ad infinitum*—mean that we naturally tend to specialize in something, to focus on what we do best.

In a market economy, this allows us to specialize in what we do best, *and get paid for it*, and then trade with other "specialists" for the goods and services we desire. An obvious consequence of this is that a capitalist economy creates an interconnected community that constantly strives to supply all of us with the best goods and services at the lowest price; it provides employment for people of all imaginable talents and abilities; it blows past subsistence economies (where one individual or family or village has to do everything itself); it creates wealth (which can support charity); and it encourages international trade, because not only are human beings unique, but so are their material and geographical resources. No government program, for instance, can ever change the fact that Saudi Arabia is a vast desert with huge supplies of oil, or that the American Midwest contains millions of acres of some of the most fertile farmland on earth. The Saudis specialize in oil and sell it to Americans; Americans specialize in agriculture and sell food to the Saudis whose irrigation systems, as sophisticated as they are, still render agricultural production several times more expensive than what can be achieved by American farmers. The international division of labor, as much as a domestic division of labor, results in everyone becoming more prosperous. Another point is that the division of labor (and knowledge) has always spawned a different kind of human cooperation in the form of teamwork, for many tasks cannot be performed by single individuals. Hence, people tend to become specialists not only in some skill or trade, but also as members of a team that produces goods and services. The division of labor and the pursuit of profit encourage human *cooperation*.

In a market economy people are paid, and businesses earn profits (or incur losses) strictly according to how good a job they do in meeting consumer demand. A good definition of capitalism in this regard would be: "Give me that which I want, and I will give you that which you want."

Inequalities of income are inevitable because of competition—some businesses and entrepreneurs do better than others. The key point, though, is that the market is fluid. Businesses can change or improve; workers can find more profitable enterprises or better ways to apply their skills.

To socialists, it is not just generic "inequality" that is wrong and has to be eliminated by government, there is also the so-called "Iron Law of Oligarchy." This is the insight that in every organization or activity, a few people will typically emerge as the leaders or top producers. Thomas Jefferson called this the phenomenon of a "natural aristocracy." We see it with "elite" athletes in professional sports; "top-of-the-chart" musicians and entertainers; Fortune 500 companies; lists of the top one hundred doctors, lawyers, or schools; and so forth. In a market economy, such "elite" individuals and institutions can demand higher wages or tuitions or whatever than the average. To most of us, there is nothing wrong with this. But socialists, and sometimes mere bureaucrats, often think differently.

The great H. L. Mencken noted that all governments, not just explicitly socialist ones, are enemies of the most energetic, productive, and motivated. In his words:

> All government, in its essence, is a conspiracy against the superior man: its one permanent object is to oppress him and cripple him. If it be aristocratic in organization, then it seeks to protect the man who is superior only in law against the man who is superior in fact; if it be democratic, then it seeks to protect the man who is inferior in every way against both. One of its primary functions is to regiment men by force, to

make them as much alike as possible and as dependent upon one another as possible, to search out and combat originality among men. All it can see in an original idea is potential change, and hence an invasion of its prerogatives. The most dangerous man to any government is the man who is able to think things out for himself, without regard to the prevailing superstitions and taboos.[4]

This is because government justifies itself by regulations, and regulations seek to impose uniformity and government control. Almost every government intervention in the economic sphere is, in reality, an attack on the natural division of labor and knowledge—the glue that holds human civilization together—in favor of a bureaucratic diktat. Every minimum wage/maximum hour law, "progressive" income tax, welfare state program, labor regulation, employment quota, tax on dividend income, special corporation income tax, and on and on, whittles away at the societal benefits of the division of labor in the forever-failing attempts to use governmental force to achieve the holy grail of material equality.

Karl Marx, the most famous of socialism's founding fathers, harshly condemned the division of labor

and the inequality it produced, and sought to eliminate it precisely in order to *destroy* existing societies
so that they could be replaced by presumed Communist utopias. Marx and Marxian socialists sought (and
seek) to use the coercive powers of government to
stamp out all human differences, differences that
Marx himself called a "contradiction" of the socialist
ideal. In Marx's own words, an ideal communist society is one:

> ...where nobody has one exclusive sphere
> of activity but each can become accom-
> plished in any branch he wishes, society
> regulates the general production and thus
> makes it possible for me to do one thing
> today and another tomorrow, to hunt in
> the morning, fish in the afternoon, rear
> cattle in the evening, criticize after dinner,
> just as I have a mind, without ever becom-
> ing a hunter, fisherman, shepherd or critic.[5]

Your author once asked a class of undergraduate
economic students what they thought of this passage.
A young man who was born and raised in Taiwan, in
the shadow of Communist China, blurted out: "Only
a child could believe such a thing!" This idea of
Marx's (and of many other prominent socialists) is the

basis for the idea of communes, where everyone is supposedly equal. Such thinking is occasionally on display in the academic world, such as when a Marxian-minded segment of the Harvard faculty traded jobs for a day with the janitorial staff.

Socialist icon Leon Trotsky predicted that once socialism had destroyed the division of labor: "[M]an will become incomparably stronger, wiser, finer. His body more harmonious, his movements more rhythmical, his voice more musical…. The human average will rise to the level of an Aristotle, a Goethe, a Marx."[6] Only a child (or infantile-minded adult) could believe such a thing.

One thing that fuels the socialist mindset—indeed, the thing that defines one as a socialist—is the overriding importance of envy, one of the seven deadly sins. Ludwig von Mises catalogued several reasons for socialists' compulsive envy in his book *The Anticapitalistic Mentality*.[7] First, there is the fact that so many people refuse to accept the reality that those who accumulate wealth in a capitalist society do so simply by pleasing large numbers of their fellow citizens with the products or services that they sell. In terms of making money, Mises wrote, "the movie star outstrips the philosopher." This often creates a lifelong feeling of envy and hatred towards capitalism and capitalists in the mind of the "philosopher." Many people also insist that they should be judged by some kind of absolute standard (defined by the government, of course) as opposed to the dollar "votes" of their fellow citizens. Consequently, they are frustrated and envious of the more successful among them. The less successful (including the lazy or incompetent) often express "hate and enmity against all those who superseded them," wrote Mises. Political demagogues take advantage of such people by promising them something for nothing ("free" health care! "free" education! "free" you name it!) in the name of egalitarianism.

Some people face up to, deal with, and improve upon their inadequacies, while others search for scapegoats. Perhaps the most popular scapegoats of all are "greedy capitalists" who are often accused of doing well financially by some nefarious, unscrupulous, or illegal means. There are of course people like this, but it is not a general characteristic of markets. There are sinners in all walks of life, not just the business world; and in a market economy (as opposed to a socialist, government-monopoly economy, where bribes are often a fact of life), no one wants to do business with dishonest people, so the market penalizes the cheaters, and products with bad reputations don't get purchased. Moreover, to preserve the integrity of markets, a market-friendly society always has laws against fraud. But envy is a powerful emotion, and so is fear, even among the wealthy and successful. Mises offered an intriguing analysis of why so many in the entertainment industry, for instance, are egalitarian socialists. Entertainers, he noted, serve consumers whose tastes can be "capricious and unaccountable." Consequently, many actors, directors, and movie producers are "rich and famous one morning and may be forgotten the next day."[8] This inherent instability of fame and fortune is what makes so many in the entertainment industry so critical of capitalism and so embracing of socialism, even though it is the freedom of capitalism that makes them rich and famous in the first place.

A similar phenomenon exists in the literary world where "trash novels" outsell serious works of nonfiction by many orders of magnitude. "The tycoon of the book market is the author of fiction for the masses," Mises observed.[9] This breeds resentment among intellectuals who write nonfiction books that languish on university library shelves. They tend to blame this "inequity" on the "unfairness" of capitalism.

But it is not "inequity" and "unfairness" that are at the root of socialist envy, it is a desire to stamp out diversity, to enforce uniformity, to order society and the economy on "rationalist" lines as designated by allegedly smarter-than-thou bureaucrats. The result, as history has shown, is often tyranny of an almost unimaginable ferocity.

Numerous writers have understood this and written about it, sometimes very entertainingly. For example, in *Facial Justice* the British fiction writer L. P. Hartley wrote of an imaginary utopia where envy is institution- alized by a government program that makes sure that all female faces are equal, performing coerced surgery to detract from the more beautiful and uplift the less attractive until "facial justice" is finally realized.[10]

Kurt Vonnegut Jr. wrote the short story "Harrison Bergeron" depicting a comprehensively egalitarian utopia:

> The year was 2081, and everyone was finally equal. They weren't only equal before God and the law. They were equal in every which way. Nobody was smarter than anybody else. Nobody was better looking than any- one else. Nobody was stronger or quicker than anybody else. All this equality was due to the 211th, 212th, and 213th Amendments to the Constitution, and to the unceasing vigilance of agents of the United States Handicapper General.[11]

The "handicapping" worked as follows: "Hazel had a perfectly average intelligence, which meant she couldn't think about anything except in short bursts.

And George, while his intelligence was way above normal, had a little mental handicap radio in his ear. He was required by law to wear it at all times. It was tuned to a government transmitter. Every twenty seconds or so, the transmitter would send out some sharp noise to keep people like George from taking unfair advantage of their brains."[12]

Egalitarianism has been lampooned in horror fiction, wrote economist Murray Rothbard, because "when the implications of such a world are fully spelled out, we recognize that such a world and such attempts are profoundly antihuman; being antihuman in the deepest sense, the egalitarian goal is, therefore, evil and any attempts in the direction of such a goal must be considered as evil as well."[13]

4

ISLANDS OF SOCIALISM: THE FOLLIES OF GOVERNMENT "ENTERPRISE"

There are degrees of socialism just as there are degrees of capitalism. Even the Soviet Union was not 100 percent socialist because it permitted a small percentage of farmland to be privately owned (the Russian Communists understood that without private property in agriculture they could never produce enough food to feed their population). There were also pervasive black markets or an "underground economy" in the Soviet Union, small islands of capitalism that allowed many to live above subsistence levels.

Today, every democratic country has islands of socialism in a sea of capitalism—government-run enterprises like the U.S. Postal Service, state and local government public works departments, police, fire-fighters, garbage collection, schools, electric, natural gas, and water utilities, transportation services, financial institutions like Fannie Mae, and dozens more. Indeed, many functions that are routinely performed by private businesses are also done by government-run enterprises.

Decades of research in economics (and simple experience) show that government-run enterprises are, as a rule, vastly more inefficient, and offer products or services of far worse quality than private businesses.[1] Economists have a "Bureaucratic Rule of Two," which holds that the per-unit cost of a government service will be on average twice as high as a comparable service offered in the competitive private sector.[2]

In a free market economy, businesses that do a good job of giving the people what they want at competitive prices are rewarded with profits. If they fail at that task they are penalized with losses or bankruptcy. This is known as the "survivor principle": businesses that fail to satisfy enough customers will not survive.

No such mechanism exists in government enterprises, for there are no profit-and-loss statements, in an accounting sense, there are only budgets.

In the private sector, profits reveal what value a business has contributed to the economy or to society. For instance, if a business takes $10,000 worth of resources and creates products for which people pay $100,000, then it has created $90,000 worth of value to society. Government enterprises, by contrast, can actually *destroy* value by using resources in a less than efficient or profitable way.

Indeed, in government, the *worse* a government agency performs, the *more* money it can claim from a legislature, city council, or county commission. If state-run schools fail to educate children, then obviously they need more money (even if government-run schools often already spend several times more per student than private schools do). If the welfare state fails to reduce, or actually increases, poverty then obviously, say the bureaucrats, we need to expand welfare programs even further. The Obama administration actually bragged about expanding food stamp rolls and claimed they were good for the economy.[3]

The socialist enterprises of federal, state, and local governments are paid for by taxpayer subsidies. Failure to pay taxes, or to pay less than what the government demands, leads to heavy fines, government confiscation of property, and/or imprisonment.

In the private sector, by contrast, there is no forcible payment, and businessmen, investing in their own businesses, have to create and market products and services that consumers want and will buy of their own free will (which also means at a reasonable price).

Government bureaucrats, at best, monopolize services that were once provided by the private sector and, in doing so, increase the cost and reduce the quality. Often they do worse than that, creating taxpayer-financed boondoggles for which there was never any real consumer demand in the first place but mere bureaucratic whim.

All of this is why the words "bureaucrat" and "bureaucratic" have taken on such negative connotations. No one likes to be called a bureaucrat, but that is what government employees are, with the well-earned reputation of having "all the efficiency of the Post Office and all the compassion of the IRS."

We are told that when government provides a service it is free, but of course nothing is free, because someone has to pay all the government employees, their overhead, and everything else that government does, buys, or appropriates. That "someone" is of course the taxpayers. Whenever socialist-minded politicians speak of "free" services, what they really mean is that the cost of the service will be hidden in taxes.

Unfortunately, hiding costs this way often works— at least for politicians, who can claim to have delivered services, but to the detriment of the public that is supposed to be served. When people are fooled into thinking something is free, they tend to want more of it. The result is shortages, overcrowding, and rationing.[4] You often hear about healthcare being rationed in socialist healthcare systems. But rationing can also be seen in situations like the periodic droughts in California. Droughts, of course, are a natural phenomenon, but governments often make them worse when government bureaucrats set water prices and allocate water usage. In 2015, California Governor Jerry Brown ordered city and county governments to enforce a reduction in water usage by 25 percent. Failure to do so would result in a $10,000 *per day* fine.[5] This comes from a state that during the concurrent drought pumped several million acre feet of fresh water *into the ocean* in pursuit of government-mandated environmental goals.[6]

Politicians sometimes try to reassure a skeptical public by saying that a state-controlled enterprise will be run "on a business-like basis."[7] But no government function can ever be run like a real business, because there is no profit and loss.

Unlike private businesses, government enterprises, supported by the taxpayers, can last for generations providing shoddy services at extremely high costs.

More than that, their tax dollar subsidies (and government regulation) can help them cripple or eliminate private-sector competition, which is one reason why the government has so many monopolies or near-monopolies. It doesn't matter if your own kids go to a private school; you still have to pay taxes for the public schools—and for the Department of Housing and Urban Development, government-run utilities, and everything else government does.

Bureaucrats do not advance in their careers through entrepreneurship, innovation, improving quality, and lowering costs. Their success is based, as economist Murray Rothbard pointed out, on *political* skills. The free market "promotes and rewards the skills of production and voluntary cooperation; government enterprise promotes the skills of mass coercion and bureaucratic submission."[8]

With its access to the taxpayer's purse and, at the federal level, its printing press known as "the Fed," government is able to pay its employees significantly more than comparable private-sector employees. According to the U.S. Bureau of Labor Statistics, state and local government employees earn 35 percent higher wages and 69 percent greater benefits than private industry employees.[9] In addition, they typically have far better job security as well; civil service regulations and the power of public employee unions make it difficult if not virtually impossible in some states to fire public employees. Even during the "Great Recession" of 2008, in many states private sector employment plummeted while government employment *expanded*.[10] Government thus provides perverse incentives for workers to leave the productive, wealth-creating private sector for the wealth-absorbing, taxpayer-funded public sector.

COST-MAXIMIZING GOVERNMENT ENTERPRISES

To be competitive, private companies have to minimize costs and continually innovate, creating new and better products. In this way, they maximize profits; and higher profits mean higher salaries, promotions, and success. Government bureaucrats don't deal with profits, they deal with budgets; and the goal is to expand the budget.[11]

Even if a government enterprise is managed by purely well-meaning, ethical bureaucrats, it still needs a bigger budget to do more "good." Every government bureaucrat is therefore a relentless lobbyist for higher taxes and more money for his or her government agency. He is, in other words, an inveterate cost *maximizer*. The fact that most government enterprises have little or no competition means that they also suffer from managerial laziness and ineptitude compared to private businesses that face competition.

Government agencies are notorious not only for wild spending binges at the end of every budget year (in order to justify more funding) and for over-staffing (a great way to spend money year after year), but for *promoting* incompetent government employees to another agency or division in a different location because of the near impossibility of firing them. If you've ever wondered why many government agencies have warehouses full of spare furniture, or why there are always twelve road repairmen standing around while four others are working, or why so many teachers grumble about the extraordinary number of overpaid school administrators, this is why. In government, waste and inefficiency is good, failure is success, and incompetence is rewarded.

For politicians, taxpayer-funded programs are *benefits* and ways of buying votes. Likewise, expanding the number of taxpayer-funded federal, state, and local employees is a form of patronage. Politicians who support public employee unions get public employee votes (and union funding).

But the general public would be a lot better off—materially and otherwise—if government shrank and more people lived not off of the taxpayer's dime, but off of their own efforts to create better products and services that people will actually pay for of their own free will. That's how real economic, and human, progress is made.

5

WHY "THE WORST" RISE TO THE TOP UNDER SOCIALISM

Perhaps the defining characteristic of socialism is the governmental imposition of one plan for all of society. Socialism is nothing if it is not "planning." This is not to say that socialism introduces the idea of planning into society. Every human being plans his way through life, day in and day out. We all plan our family lives, our work days, our education, our career paths, our children's future. Socialism is *the forceful substitution of governmental plans for individual plans*. Hence, it does not really matter if it is imposed on a society by a majority-rule democracy or a totalitarian dictatorship. In either case everyone in society is subjected to the coercive forces of the state in enforcing *its* plans for the whole society. "Obamacare" will have the same effect on American society whether it was imposed by democratic politics or by a dictator.

In his classic book *The Road to Serfdom*, Friedrich Hayek explained that because "collectivism" of all kinds, including socialism, necessarily involves the coerced imposition of some governmental plan (or plans) on the population, such a system attracts as its political leaders some of the most immoral and unethical people in society. For once the governmental plans are in place and begin to fail, as they inevitably will because of all the inherent economic weaknesses of socialism that we've already touched on, then "the democratic statesman who sets out to plan economic life will soon be confronted with the alternative of either assuming dictatorial powers or abandoning his plans" and admitting failure.[1] He would "soon have to choose between disregard of ordinary morals and failure. It is for this reason that the unscrupulous and uninhibited are likely to be more successful" in a socialist society seeking to impose government planning of more and more aspects of its citizens' lives.[2]

Those with the least qualms about depriving their fellow citizens of their civil liberties, or even brutalizing and abusing them, will rise to the top of such a society. This was in fact the history of twentieth-century socialism all around the world. Socialism, wrote Hayek, inevitably led to "the suppression of democratic institutions" and the movement toward a more dictatorial or totalitarian government.

Democratic socialism is, then, something of a non-sequitur. Socialists might be elected democratically, but their entire government program relies on government displacing the authority of individuals or families or private institutions or even constitutional restrictions on government power. A significant movement in this direction has already taken place in the United States with the expansion of federal executive powers, the proliferation of "executive orders" by presidents, and the creation of dozens of presidentially appointed "czars" to plan and regulate everything from air travel to energy to weapons of mass destruction.[3] How appropriate that these largely unaccountable presidential appointees (the "czars") with immense regulatory powers are named after the notoriously repressive and authoritarian Russian monarchy (that was, of course, displaced by the even more totalitarian Communists).

Because of the inevitable failure of socialist bureaucrats to "plan" an economy and a society better than the millions of individuals comprising the society can, there will be "dissatisfaction with the slow and cumbersome course of democratic procedure which makes action for action's sake the goal," wrote Hayek.[4] "It is then the man or the party who seems strong and resolute enough 'to get things done' who exercises the greatest appeal" to the public.[5] The public demands a "strongman" (or strongwoman) "who can get things done"—even if it means the abandonment of democracy. Writing in 1943, Hayek was obviously referring to the national socialist "strongman" Adolf Hitler, but there have been many other examples, especially in Latin America.

Once such a leader is empowered, he will want to surround himself with "a group which is prepared voluntarily to submit to that totalitarian discipline which they are to impose by force on the rest."[6] The history of socialism in the twentieth century, Hayek reminded his readers, demonstrated that only the "ruthless ready to disregard the barriers of accepted morals" could execute the socialist program of pervasive governmental "planning."

Moreover, the socialist regime is likely to be populated by "the worst elements of any society," warned Hayek. Political demagogues (and socialists are always demagogues) have long understood that it is easier for the masses to agree on a *negative* program—a hatred of an enemy or "the envy of the better off" than on any positive program.[7] In Bolshevik Russia, it was the capitalists and monarchists and Christians and independent farmers and aristocrats who were the enemy, and against whom the masses could be swayed, and against whom violence could be inflicted in the name of "the people." In the Europe of Hayek's day it was the plutocrat and "the Jew who became the enemy...."[8] "In Germany and Austria the Jew had come to be regarded as the representative of capitalism," and hence became the target of extreme hatred.[9] In America, political demagogues target "Wall Street" and the wealthy "one percent" as the objects of *their* hatred.

Hatred and violence, especially for the young, is justified in the name of idealism, however perversely understood. To a socialist, the ends justify the means (which is the reverse of traditional morality) and can justify *any* action desired by a socialist. To a socialist, said Hayek, there is nothing "which the consistent collectivist must not be prepared to do if it serves 'the good of the whole.'"[10] This socialist mindset accepts if not celebrates "intolerance and brutal suppression of dissent," and "the complete disregard of the life and happiness of the individual,"[11] because the "selfish" individual does not matter; the socialist will argue that what he does is "for the good of the whole."

In a socialist society, said Hayek, the only "power" worth having is political power, and to consolidate that political power government relies on propaganda, intimidation, and government domestic spying to discredit, bully, and eliminate possible opposition.

Socialism can lead to "the end of truth," as Hayek called it, because socialists believe in indoctrinating people into "The Truth." This is why socialist regimes have made us familiar with "reeducation camps" and rigid, totalitarian ideological conformity. Socialists believe that there are no legitimate, alternative viewpoints. Socialist propaganda must dominate the educational system and the mass media so that, in Hayek's words, "a pseudoscientific theory becomes part of the official creed" which "directs everybody's actions."[12] Under socialism, "every act of the government, must become sacrosanct," while minority opinions—or even majority opinions at odds with the official ideology—must be silenced and are demonized.[13] This all sounds like a perfect definition of the "political correctness" that plagues American colleges and universities and which has gone a long way toward destroying academic freedom both for students and professors.

"Truth" in a socialist society is not something to be debated; it is mandated and enforced by the Socialist regime, from which there is no alternative and no appeal. Once socialist ideology takes over and respect for *actual* truth is destroyed, wrote Hayek, then *all* morals are assaulted because all morality is based on respect for the truth.

THE WORST OF THE WORST UNDER SOCIALISM

To young people, the Cold War seems like ancient history; and they are increasingly unaware that Communist regimes deliberately killed tens of millions of their own citizens. These are not war deaths, but deliberate acts of mass murder of civilians *by their own governments*. These crimes were catalogued in *The Black Book of Communism*, edited by several French intellectuals and published by Harvard University Press in English in 1999.[14] Their summary statistics include the following death counts:

USSR: 20 million deaths

China: 60 million deaths

Vietnam: 1 million deaths

North Korea: 2 million deaths

Cambodia: 2 million deaths

Eastern Europe: 1 million deaths

Latin America: 150,000 deaths

Africa: 1.7 million deaths

Afghanistan: 1.5 million deaths

The total estimated number of people murdered by socialist regimes in the twentieth century is nearly one hundred million. Among the techniques employed by socialist regimes were: "firing squads, hanging, drowning, battering…gassing, poisoning or 'car accidents'; destruction of the population by starvation, through man-made famine, the withholding of food, or both; deportation, through which death can occur in transit…or through forced labor (exhaustion, illness, hunger, cold)."[15] The Soviet Union's "experiment" with socialism included what these authors call "its venture into planned, logical, and 'politically-correct' mass slaughter."[16]

Although fascism will be discussed in the next chapter, it is worth pointing out here that fascism was a type of socialism. The Nazis called themselves "national" socialists, to distinguish themselves from their fellow socialists in Russia who labeled themselves *international* socialists. The German national socialists of the early twentieth century murdered approximately "21 million men, women, handicapped, aged, sick, prisoners of war, forced laborers, camp inmates, critics, homosexuals, Jews, Slavs, Serbs, Czechs, Italians, Poles, Frenchmen, Ukrainians…. Among them were 1 million children under eighteen years of age," according to sociologist R.J. Rummel, who spent his entire academic career documenting "democide," or death by government.[17]

Socialist "ideology and absolute power are the critical variables in Soviet democide," wrote Hummel. "They explain how individual communists could beat, torture, and murder by the hundreds, and sleep well at night. Grim tasks, to be sure, but after all, they were working for the greater good," he wrote sarcastically, echoing Hayek.[18]

Russia's "international socialists" were very egalitarian in their mass murdering of any and all who might be suspected of having doubts about the glories of their socialist Nirvana. As Rummel explained:

> Some [of the socialists' victims] were from the wrong class—bourgeoisie, landowners, aristocrats, kulaks. Some were from the wrong nation or race—Ukrainians, Black Sea Greeks, Kalmyks, Volga Germans. Some were from the wrong political faction—Trotskyites, Mensheviks, Social Revolutionaries. Some were just their sons and daughters, wives and husbands, or mothers and fathers. And some were in lands occupied by the Red Army—Balts, Germans, Poles, Hungarians, Rumanians. Then some were simply in the way of social progress, like the mass of peasants or religious believers. And some were eliminated because of their potential opposition, such as writers, teachers, churchmen; or the military high command....[19]

The Soviet government actually had a system of quotas handed down to its functionaries and henchmen. Rummel quotes Vladimir Petrov, a Soviet spy who defected in the 1950s, who revealed a written order once given to him saying: "You are charged with the task of exterminating 10,000 enemies of the people. Report results by signal."[20]

When the Soviets weren't committing acts of mass murder, they were involved in the sadistic torture of those suspected of being potential political dissenters. One Polish citizen who was imprisoned by the Soviets wrote in his memoir of how he was beaten with a hard-rubber truncheon, whipped, had his hair torn, endured cigarette burns, had his fingers burned, was deprived of sleep for nine days, and worse.[21]

Torture and murder were the foundations of government power in the socialist Soviet empire. Things were even worst in Mao's China. The Chinese Communists killed three times the number of people killed by the Soviet Union—and again, these were China's own people, the eggs that allegedly had to be broken to make the Communist omelet. How remarkable it is that to this day, self-proclaimed socialists in academe claim to occupy the moral high ground. The ideology that is associated with the worst crimes, the greatest mass slaughters, the most totalitarian regimes *ever,* is allegedly more compassionate than the free market capitalism that has lifted more people from poverty, created more wealth, provided more opportunities for human development, and supported human freedom more than any other economic system in the history of the world.

Socialism has not yet reached a critical stage in the United States, but the more a society moves in the direction of socialism, the more it relies on the coercive powers of the state. As such coercion becomes justified, it tends to expand at the expense of individual freedom and individual conscience. Government plans replace individual plans; the government claims a greater share of private wealth to distribute money as it sees fit; ideological propaganda becomes more pervasive from government institutions, especially in the schools; and the economy becomes progressively more lethargic, increasingly strangled by governmental edicts, regulations, and bureaucrats. Government becomes more and more a government of the worst, by the worst, and for the worst. That's what socialism delivers.

6

THE SOCIALIST ROOTS OF FASCISM

There are few words in the English language that have as negative a connotation as "fascism." The word brings to mind the horrors of Nazi Germany, Japanese imperialism during the first half of the twentieth century, and Hitler's ally, the Italian dictator Mussolini. After World War II the socialist dictator of the Soviet Union, Joseph Stalin, engineered a rhetorical/propaganda coup (with the help of the worldwide socialist movement) by repeating the notion that the only alternative to Russian socialism was fascism. Classical liberalism, with its emphasis on individual freedom, free-market economics, peace, and constitutionalism was treated as though it never existed; indeed, it was conflated with one of its deadliest enemies and opponents, fascism. But as we've seen, socialists are never much concerned about truth.

The truth is that fascism was always a form of *socialism*. Benito Mussolini, the founder of fascist Italy, had been an *international* socialist before a *national* socialist, the latter being the essence of fascism. Nationalist socialism was also content to allow private business to survive as long as it was directed by government subsidies and policy, a form of socialist control that in our own country goes by the name of "crony capitalism," where government rewards its political friends rather than allowing the operation of a free market.

In 2007 the University of Chicago Press published Hayek's *The Road to Serfdom* as volume two of *The Collected Works of F.A. Hayek*, edited by economist Bruce Caldwell.[1] This version of the book included several appendices, including a 1933 essay that Hayek wrote entitled "Nazi-Socialism." "[T]he socialist character of National Socialism [Nazism] has been quite generally unrecognized," Hayek wrote.[2] German businessmen who supported the Nazi Party were incredibly shortsighted, said Hayek, for they did not recognize the pervasive anti-capitalism that was at the heart of national socialism.

Referring to the economic policy positions of the Nazi Party (as opposed to its militarism and anti-Semitism) Hayek noted that the Nazi policy platform was "full of ideas resembling those of the early socialists."[3] The dominant feature, he said, was a fierce hatred of anything capitalistic—"individual profit seeking, large-scale enterprise, banks, joint-stock companies, department stores, international finance and loan capital, the system of 'interest slavery,' in general...."[4]

Hayek described the Nazi policy program as nothing less than a "violent anti-capitalistic attack," which is not at all surprising since "It is not even denied [in 1933] that many of the young men who today play a prominent part in it have previously been communists or socialists."[5] Moreover, the common characteristic of all the German journalists at the time who supported the Nazis "was their anti-liberal and anti-capitalist trend"; they even adopted the slogan "the end of capitalism" as their "accepted dogma."[6]

One distinguishing feature of German national socialism, as opposed to Russian international socialism, was that it purported to be "middle class socialism" as opposed to proletarian socialism. All of the "leading men," in Italian and German fascism, Hayek point out, "from Mussolini downward.... began as socialists and ended as Fascists or Nazis."[7]

FASCISM AS A VARIETY OF SOCIALISM

As with all forms of socialism, fascist ideology was first and foremost an attack on classical liberalism, the philosophy that underpins capitalism, and that was perhaps stated clearest in Ludwig von Mises' 1927 book *Liberalism*.[8] The key features of classical liberalism, as defined by Mises, are property rights, freedom, peace, equality under the law, acceptance of the inequality of income and wealth based on the reality of human uniqueness, limited constitutional government, and tolerance.

Socialism in all its varieties is nothing if it is not an attack on every one of these principles, especially private property. Indeed, "THE ABOLITION OF PRIVATE PROPERTY" is the hallmark idea of *The Communist Manifesto*. Socialist ideologues and propagandists like Benito Mussolini spent years crusading against the principles of classical liberalism and capitalism to lay the ideological groundwork for their brand of socialism. In his book, *Fascism: Doctrine and Institutions*, Mussolini wrote that "The Fascist conception of life stresses the importance of the State and accepts the individual only in so far as his interests coincide with the State.... *It is opposed to classical liberalism*... [which] denied the State in the name of the individual" (emphasis added).[9]

The second chapter of *The Road to Serfdom* compares and contrasts the philosophies of collectivism, which is socialism in all its variants, and individualism, defined simply as respect for the individual as an individual. Human beings own themselves, the individualist philosophy contends, and should not be viewed as pawns in political chess games operated by politicians, or as human "rats" to be experimented upon by social engineers. Socialists believe exactly the opposite. As expressed by Mussolini himself: "The maxim that society exists only for the well-being and freedom of the individuals composing it does not seem to be in conformity with nature's plans, which care only for the species and seem ready to sacrifice the individual."[10] This idea that individuals can be and should be sacrificed for "the greater good" is the essence of the fascist/socialist/collectivist philosophy.

Mussolini declared classical liberal ideas to be dead when he pontificated that "if the XIXth century was the century of the individual (liberalism implies individualism) we are free to believe that this is the 'collective' century, and therefore the century of the State.... If classical liberalism spells individualism, Fascism spells government."[11]

Like Marx and Engels in *The Communist Manifesto*, Mussolini harshly denounced capitalism and free markets. He bemoaned "the selfish pursuit of material prosperity"; declared fascism to be a "reaction…against the flaccid materialistic conception of happiness"; and implored his audiences to "reject the economistic literature of the 18th century,"[12] presumably referring to the free market writings of Adam Smith.

Italian and German fascists nationalized many, but not all, industries. They allowed a much larger degree of private property ownership and private business ownership than the Russian socialists did, but the key was that private business was to be heavily regulated and regimented so that it operated in "the interests of the Nation as a whole," as defined by the government. As explained by the Italian fascist apologist Fausto Pitigliani: "The function of private enterprise is assessed from the standpoint of public interest, and hence an owner or director of a business undertaking is responsible before the State for his production policy."[13]

Thus, Italian fascism was an assault on private property and private enterprise, only in a slightly different form than under Russian socialism. Both forms of socialism advocated pervasive government planning of the economy and society. Pitigliani called for a government "plan which comprises the harmonious gradations of the economic life of the nation,"[14] whatever that means, while Mussolini promised that centralized government planning would "introduce order in the economic field,"[15] as opposed to the supposed "chaos" of capitalism. Consequently, the Mussolini regime established government regulatory agencies that dictated orders to every business, every industry, and every labor union, all in the name of governmental "coordination." It achieved the basic aims of socialism—government *control* of the means of production—while leaving corporate managers in place. Government control, of course, means taxpayers foot the bill. As Italian writer Gaetano Salvemini explained in his book, *Under the Axe of Fascism*: "In December 1932 a fascist financial expert…estimated that more than 8.5 billion Lira had been paid out by the government from 1923 to 1932 in order to help depressed industries. From December 1932 to 1935 the outlay must have doubled."[16] Massive government regulation and taxpayer bailouts of failing favored industries meant that Italian fascism, like every other form of socialism, was an economic failure.

GERMAN NATIONAL SOCIALISM

German fascists, like their Italian allies and Communist rivals, waged a relentless propaganda campaign against classical liberalism and capitalism. One of the intellectual fathers of German fascism was Paul Lensch, who wrote in his book *Three Years of World Revolution:*

> This class of people, who unconsciously reason from English standards, comprises the whole German Bourgeoisie. Their political notions of 'freedom' and 'civic right,' of constitutionalism and parliamentarianism, are derived from that individualistic conception of the world, of which English liberalism is a classical embodiment, and which was adopted by the spokesmen of the German bourgeoisie in the 'fifties, 'sixties and 'seventies of the nineteenth century. But these standards are old fashioned and shattered, just as old-fashioned English liberalism has been shattered.... What has to be done now is to get rid of these inherited political ideas and to assist in the growth of a new conception of State and Society. In this sphere also Socialism must present a conscious and determined opposition to individualism.[17]

By "English standards," Lensch meant the ideas of such men as Adam Smith and John Locke. German fascism, like all collectivist ideologies, held that individuals must serve "the community" as defined by the state. As Hitler wrote in *Mein Kampf*: "The Aryan is not greatest in his mental qualities as such, but in the extent of his willingness to put all his abilities in the service of the community.... He willingly subordinates his own ego to the community and, if the hour demands, even sacrifices it."[18] This was the basic philosophy of the National Socialist German Workers Party, expressed under the slogan, "The Common Good Comes before the Private Good."

Like Mussolini and the Russian socialists, Hitler condemned "hyper-individualism" in particular and capitalism in general. The individual was said to have no rights, only duties to the state. "The Official 25-Point Program of the Nazi Party," published in 1925, laid this out.[19] It insisted that "the activities of the individual must not clash with the interests of the whole, but must proceed within the framework of the community and must be for the general good." Of course, Hitler would decide for all Germans what constituted "the general good." In Soviet Russia it would be Stalin, and in Italy Mussolini. The Nazi Program announced: "We demand ruthless war upon all those whose activities are injurious to the common interest." This included "usurers" and "profiteers" who "must be punished with death...."

The Nazi Program condemned private banking by calling for "the abolition of the slavery of interest" and called for the socialization of land "without compensation" and the "prohibition of all speculation in land." The Nazi Program stated: "We demand the education of…children…at the expense of the State." All schools were to be turned into national socialist indoctrination academies.

Jews were singled out as personifying the hated and despised capitalist system that the Nazis wanted to destroy. "The party…combats the Jewish-materialist spirit within and without us, and is convinced that our nation can achieve permanent health from within only on the principle: the common interest before self-interest." Among the other "demands" were "abolition of unearned incomes"; "breaking of debt slavery"; "the nationalization of all associated industries"; and "an expansion on a large scale of old age welfare." Children were to be indoctrinated in socialist philosophy "as early as the beginning of understanding"; and the media were to be under strict government control to prevent "known lies" about fascism. There was certainly nothing capitalistic about any of this.

Much of this was also in *The Communist Manifesto*, which is not surprising since, as Hayek pointed out, all of the early fascist theorists were first and foremost socialists or had been Communists. *The*

Communist Manifesto, published in 1848, contained a ten-point Communist Platform that called for abolishing the private ownership of land and the nationalization of industry. The German and Italian fascists did not abolish all private property or nationalize all of the means of production, but the Germans nationalized about half of the German economy, according to Hayek, and then took effective control of the rest of it through extensive and pervasive regulation and regimentation of all industry and agriculture, just as Italy had done under Mussolini.

The Communist Manifesto also called for "Centralizing credit in the banks of the state," which the Nazis did, as well as government control of "the means of communication...." The Nazi Program and *The Communist Manifesto* demanded an "obligation" for all to work at jobs approved of or prescribed by the state. And of course both advocated some form of what the *Manifesto* called "Free education for all children in public schools." The educational system had to be nationalized and centralized so as to prevent criticisms of socialism, however it was defined.

Perhaps the biggest commonality between Russian, Italian, and German socialism during the twentieth century was the creation of a highly centralized bureaucratic state that eradicated political power at the state and local levels. As stated in the final, twenty-fifth point of the Nazi Party Program, "we demand the formation of a strong central power in the Reich" along with "Unlimited authority of the central parliament over the whole Reich...."

Socialists, of all varieties, tolerate no opposition, allow no competing authorities, and are at continual war with individuals, families, private organizations, churches, businesses, and local and regional authorities that might oppose or interfere with their grand vision for reordering society. Socialists believe in total control. They want to control you.

7

THE MYTH OF SUCCESSFUL SCANDINAVIAN SOCIALISM

Socialists like to point to Sweden as an example of how a heavily regulated economy can out-perform a free market one. But they're wrong. Socialism nearly wrecked Sweden, and free market reforms are finally bringing its economy back from the brink of disaster.

The real source of Sweden's relatively high standard of living has nothing to do with socialism and every-thing to do with Sweden avoiding both world wars and jumping into the industrial revolution when its economy was one of the freest, least regulated, and least taxed in Europe.

Sweden's high degree of economic freedom in the late nineteenth and early twentieth centuries gave rise to many extraordinary inventors and entrepreneurs, such as Alfred Nobel, inventor of dynamite; engineer Sven Wingquist, who invented the self-aligning ball bearing; Gustaf Dalén, who founded the gas company AGA; and Baltzar von Platen, who invented the gas-absorption refrigerator. Volvo, Saab, and the telecommunications company Ericsson were also founded during this era.[1]

Thanks to its relatively free economy and its ability to avoid war (having fought no war, and diverted no resources, including "the ultimate resource," people,[2] to destruction since 1809), Sweden was able to enjoy the highest per-capita income growth *in the world* from 1870 to 1950.[3]

Starting in the 1930s, Swedish politicians became infatuated with fascist-style, socialist "planning." Fascism, of course, fell out of favor, but in the postwar era Sweden expanded its "planned, socialist society" with an ever-growing welfare state. Government spending as a percentage of Swedish GDP rose from what would today seem a relatively modest 20 percent in 1950 to more than 50 percent by 1975.[4] Taxes, public debt, and the number of government employees expanded relentlessly.[5] Swedes were, in essence, living off of the hard work, investments, and entrepreneurship of previous generations. The country remained relatively prosperous, but could not avoid economic reality. It is impossible to maintain a thriving economy with a regime of high taxes, a wasteful welfare state that pays people not to work, and massive government spending and borrowing. By the 1980s, Sweden's collapse of economic growth and a government attempt to jumpstart the economy with a massive expansion of credit resulted in economic chaos, with stock market and real estate bubbles that burst, and interest rates that the Swedish central bank pushed up to 500 percent.[6] By 1990, Sweden had fallen from fourth to twentieth place in international income comparisons.[7] This precipitous economic decline led to a revolt against the socialist regime. More conservative governments sharply reduced marginal income tax rates; abolished currency controls; deregulated bank lending; privatized several government enterprises; deregulated the retail, telecommunications, and airline industries; and implemented deep government spending cuts. But it was a long road back thanks to the incredible burden of Sweden's welfare state. A 2009 study by the Swedish Economic Association discovered that the Swedish economy had failed to create any new jobs on net from 1950 to 2005.[8] Thanks to conservative reforms, however, progress was finally being made, and Sweden's national debt went from 80 percent of GDP in 1992 to 40 percent by 2008.[9]

While conservative reforms are restoring Sweden's economy, the social and economic effects of many decades of socialism will take years to undo. For instance, so many Swedes live off of government "sick benefits" and "early retirement," that the actual unemployment rate in Sweden is probably at least three times higher than the "official" government unemployment rate. Thousands of Swedes are paid by the government to participate in "labor market political activities" whose "only purpose is to reduce the official unemployment rate."[10]

Swedish socialism has also created a new type of "socialist man." As described by Swedish economist Per Bylund, "[W]hen handing out benefits and therefore taking away the individual's responsibility for his or her own life, a new kind of individual is created— the immature, irresponsible, and dependent.... [T]he welfare state has created...a population of psychological and moral children...."[11] The children and grandchildren of the welfare state, writes Bylund (as opposed to earlier generations) are indoctrinated at an early age in the government schools that they have a supposed "right" to "free" education, health care, an income, and anything else they might desire. Of course, no one can have a "right" to such material things unless *someone else* can be *compelled* to pay for them. Generations of Swedes, however, have been taught that they have a "right" to live at someone else's expense.

They also believe that their elders—their own aged parents and grandparents—should be taken care of by someone else, namely the state. Consequently, writes Bylund, "most elderly in Sweden either live depressed and alone in their homes, waiting for death to come their way, or they have been institutionalized in public elderly collective living facilities with 24/7 surveillance so as to alleviate the burden on the younger working generations."[12]

Similarly, Swedish parents tend to believe that children "should absolutely not intrude on their parents' right to a career, long holidays abroad, and attending social events."[13] The Swedish welfare state, says Bylund, has created "egotistical monsters" by "handing out privileges and benefits to everybody at 'nobody's' expense."[14]

Despite Sweden's economic recovery after the mid-1990s, socialists might be surprised to learn that it is still poorer than Mississippi, the lowest-income state in the United States.[15] Another surprise for socialists is that Sweden has been privatizing portions of its socialized healthcare, social security, and education sectors; and private health insurance is booming because of the inevitable rationing, shortages, and long wait times of socialized healthcare.[16]

DANISH SOCIALISM, ANYONE?

Denmark is another Scandinavian country that is trying, with good reason, to flee from its socialist past. More than a quarter of the working-age population (eighteen to sixty-six) is on the government dole; for every one hundred persons employed full time, there are about sixty working-age welfare recipients.[17] More than 1.5 million people in a country of approximately 5.5 million people live *full-time* on taxpayer-funded welfare handouts. This requires a very heavy tax burden, including, using 2016 numbers, a marginal income tax rate of 55.6 percent (on incomes of $55,000 and above), a 25 percent national sales tax, and a wide variety of other taxes, including an additional 180 percent tax on automobile purchases.[18] "Green taxes" on such things as heating, electricity, water, and gasoline increased dramatically in the 1990s when the socialist Social Democrats were in power.

Danish economist Per Henrik Hansen estimates that the "total tax level…approaches 70 percent." He calls this "a relentless and debilitating" force against "personal economic achievement and…accumulation of wealth."[19]

It might be no surprise, then, that as in Sweden, many Danish voters have turned to conservative and free market parties to bring Denmark back to economic sanity. Indeed, the classical liberal Venstre

Party was in power in a coalition with the Conservative People's Party from 2001 to 2011, and was elected on its own in 2015.

The real lesson, it seems, of Scandinavian socialism is that it wrecks economies and eventually leads to the election of classical liberal and conservative parties to try to undo the damage.

8

HOW WELFARE HARMS THE POOR

Ludwig von Mises wrote that socialists had twin strategies to achieve their goals: one was nationalizing industry and property, the other was "destructionism." Mises defined "destructionism" as "destroying the social order which is based on private ownership."[1] Destructionism can be advanced through, among other means, the welfare state, high taxes, and excessive regulation. It is, for the hardened socialist, a form of social and economic sabotage. Socialists, for instance, can use the welfare state to crowd out private charity, making poor people dependent on socialist government. As Frédéric Bastiat pointed out in the mid-nineteenth century, government welfare programs are "false philanthropy," undercutting personal charity and creating the assumption that "government" will take care of that.

Professor Marvin Olasky has called this same phenomenon in the history of the United States "the tragedy of American compassion."[2] America, from its founding through the nineteenth century, was renow-ned for its proliferation of voluntary charitable organizations. Alexis de Tocqueville famously marveled at them in his 1835 book *Democracy in America.*

In the latter half of the twentieth century, however, private philanthropy was increasingly displaced by government programs, which were not only far more bureaucratic but far less effective than private charity had been. Traditional American private charities focused on helping people to help themselves. Government programs, inevitably, became much more focused on creating "clients" to justify the ever increasing number (and salaries) of bureaucrats. In the process, "compassion" no longer meant self-sacrifice for the benefit of others, but merely rhetorical support for more *government* welfare programs; welfare programs made people forget there was any other way to "help" the poor. Political scientist

Charles Murray noted in his book *In Pursuit: Of Happiness and Good Government*:

> From the beginning of the 1940s through 1964...the richer the United States got, the greater the proportion of its wealth that was given to philanthropy. Then, suddenly, sometime during 1964–65, in the middle of an economic boom, this consistent trend was reversed. The proportion of wealth being given away began to fall even though wealth continued to increase. This new and disturbing trend continued through the rest of the 1960s, throughout the 1970s....[3]

As Murray explained it, the burgeoning welfare state prompted millions of Americans to ask themselves: "Why donate $500 of your money...to a local [charity] when there is a bureaucracy in your city spending $20 million on the same thing? Why give up an evening a week...to do something for which the city has a full-time paid staff of several hundred people?"[4] However rational this might seem, wrote Murray, it had several unforeseen consequences. Not only did individuals become less involved in charity, but local charitable institutions effectively had their functions taken away. Take away the charitable functions of these institutions, churches, clubs, and whatnot, said Murray, and "you take away the community" itself. The welfare state has done a very good job of destroying voluntary neighborhood and community efforts to help the poor, rendering many low-income families dependent on government handouts not for a short while but for generations, as an entitlement, a reward for having children out of wedlock and without a job.

SUBSIDIZING POVERTY

Most economists recognize that welfare programs pose a potential "moral hazard" with "benefits," potentially destroying the incentive to find a job and become financially independent. That's why President John F. Kennedy declared that the purpose of welfare was to provide "a hand, not a handout."

Welfare policy in America, however, has failed miserably in avoiding this moral hazard. A dramatic illustration of this failure was provided by Charles Murray in his landmark book, *Losing Ground*.[5] Murray examined how the explosion of welfare benefits in the mid- and late-1960s perpetuated rather than alleviated poverty; in fact, it made it worse.

Murray found that from the 1950s until the late 1960s, thanks to America's vigorous post-war economy, the number of people living in poverty had declined by about a third.[6] But from 1968, as the massive increase in welfare benefits began, to 1980, when Ronald Reagan was elected president, poverty *increased* by 22 percent.

The poverty we're talking about is "latent poverty," which means poverty before you factor in welfare benefits. "Poverty" went up because "poverty" became attractive—or, to put it another way, welfare discouraged people from getting jobs, because the more money one earned the more one was likely to suffer reduced welfare payments, food stamps, housing subsidies, and other benefits.

In 2012, a Congressional Budget Office study found that a welfare single parent with one child who got a job faced a marginal tax rate (in terms of lost benefits) of between 66 percent and 95 percent.

A 2013 Cato Institute study found that the value of welfare benefits for a single family (taking into consideration only seven of 126 federal programs) ranged from $49,175 in Hawaii to $16,984 in Mississippi.[7] A single parent in Hawaii, or in many other states, would have to secure a very well-paying job to compensate for the loss of tens of thousands of dollars in government benefits; the government has, for many welfare families, made getting a job an irrational decision. So it should be no surprise that after spending more than $4 trillion on welfare programs since 1965, the United States has seen poverty *increase*.[8]

With welfare payments so widespread, the stigma that once attached to not working has gone away, replaced by the sense that those who do work in low-paying jobs are chumps. Murray wrote: "For the first time in American history, it became socially acceptable within poor communities to be unemployed...."[9]

Welfare programs have become an alternative to work. A 1992 study by economists Richard Vedder and Lowell Gallaway found that only 18 percent of welfare recipients moved out of poverty, compared to 45 percent of poor people who did not receive welfare.[10]

The welfare state has done an excellent job of crippling an important cornerstone of an enterprising, free market, capitalist society: the incentive to work. Instead, it has created a dependent class that it serves (with programs) and from whom it benefits (justifying government programs and jobs).

The welfare state has also gone a long way toward achieving another goal of many socialists, especially Karl Marx, of the "abolition of the family" (as Marx and Engels advocated in *The Communist Manifesto*).

This is not to say that the architects of the American welfare state *wanted* to abolish the family, only that their policies have gone a long way toward achieving it. Between 1960 and 2000, out-of-wedlock births increased by more than *400 percent*, and a big driver of that, especially in black communities, was that single parenthood brings government benefits.[11] In 1950, before "the war on poverty," about 88 percent of white families and 77 percent of black families in the United States consisted of husband-and-wife households.[12] By 1980 the proportion of black families with husband-and-wife households had declined to 59 percent; among white families it was 85 percent. And the numbers continue to get worse. In 1960, 73 percent of kids lived in a traditional two-parent family. In 2013, the number was 46 percent.[13] Single mothers are much more likely to be poor mothers; and all too often welfare payments have taken the place of a husband with a job. Just as there is no longer a stigma to accepting welfare and not working, the welfare state has removed the stigma of "illegitimacy" when so many millions of women give birth out of wedlock and receive child support not from fathers but from taxpayers.

Children born to single parents are three times more likely to suffer behavioral or emotional problems; girls are twice as likely to have children out of wedlock themselves; and boys are twice as likely to become involved in crime.[14] In other words, welfare dependency has a "domino effect" that not only harms society but also destroys people's lives.

Taking the advice of socialist politicians like Vermont Senator Bernie Sanders to vastly increase the size of the welfare state is bound to *increase* poverty; *increase* the incidence of child pathologies; *increase* the number of children who get involved in crime; *increase* human misery; and *discourage* effective, private, voluntary efforts to help the poor. No one, not even the bureaucrat, really benefits when socialism deconstructs society. In its human costs, socialism makes us all losers.

9

HOW SOCIALIZED MEDICINE KILLS THE PATIENT AND ROBS THE TAXPAYER

When it comes to something as important as healthcare, the last thing anyone should want is for the entire system to become a government-run monopoly.

Shortly before "Obamacare" became law, I received a letter from a Canadian woman praying that Americans did *not* adopt Canadian-style, socialist healthcare. She told me the story of how her six-year-old son suddenly became violently ill (she suspected appendicitis), was rushed to an emergency room, and was ignored by medical staff despite his mother's pleas.[1] A doctor finally strolled into their stark, filthy waiting room, dismissed the child's vomiting and soaring fever as "just a bug," but ordered blood tests to pacify the mother. *Six hours* later the tests revealed that the child was indeed suffering from appendicitis and was whisked away for an emergency appendectomy. The child's appendicitis was so severe that the surgeon surmised that the child was minutes from dying. It reminded the mother that she had recently read of three other people sent home from this same hospital's emergency room who had later died of appendicitis. After she shared her experience of Canada's "Soviet-style emergency rooms" on Facebook, dozens more stories appeared there, written by Canadians with similar experiences.

It is a testament to the power of government propaganda that in Britain and Canada socialized medicine is popular because it is "free"—or, in other words, hidden in taxes; and because the government runs monopolies, Canadian health care is actually far *more* expensive, and the quality far *less* than it would be if doctors and hospitals had to compete for patients on the basis of quality and price.

It is a myth, of course, but widely believed in Europe, thanks to decades of socialist propaganda, that the poor and elderly receive *no* healthcare in the United States. Federal law actually requires hospitals to treat "indigent-care patients," and Medicaid and

Medicare—themselves highly flawed socialist programs—provide coverage for lower-income and over-sixty-five Americans. These are not exactly secrets; Europe's (and Canada's) leftist politicians purposely lie about this subject in order to deceive their populations about the alleged benefits of healthcare socialism in *their* countries.

In fact, socialist healthcare is based almost entirely on deception. It works this way: patients usually pay nothing (or a miniscule fee) at the point of service, thereby forming the false impression that healthcare is "free." Because it is "free," consumer demand for healthcare skyrockets; doctors prescribe hordes of often unnecessary tests, because they are "free" to the patient. The costs of providing healthcare, including everything from nursing to ambulance services, inevitably go through the roof. This is why former Texas Senator Phil Gramm, who holds a Ph.D. in economics and taught at Texas A&M University before becoming a congressman and then a senator, said of the Clinton administration plan for healthcare socialism in the 1990s: "There's not enough money in the world to pay for it." As any freshman economics student should know, declaring *anything* to be a "free" good or service will cause an explosion of demand, which in turn will ratchet up the costs of providing the good or service.

To cover up these costs, socialist governments typically impose price ceilings on everything from doctors' visits and salaries to hospital room rates and technology. A price ceiling is a government-imposed price that is below the existing price. The effect is to stimulate the demand for healthcare services even more. Supply never catches up, generating shortages in everything from doctors to MRI machines. Indeed, after the British and Canadians socialized their healthcare industries and imposed price ceilings on doctors' salaries, there was a massive "brain drain," as highly educated medical professionals migrated to countries like the United States where they could earn a better living.

Governments always respond to the shortages *that their policies created* by imposing some kind of rationing. In Britain more than one million people are waiting to be admitted to hospitals at any one time; in Canada, one study found that 876,000 people were waiting for treatments; in Norway more than 270,000 people are daily waiting for hospital admissions and other medical treatment; and in New Zealand, some 90,000 people wait for medical care on any given day.[2]

Canadian patients waited more than eight weeks to see a specialist and then another nine-and-a-half weeks before treatment, including surgery. In New Zealand, the average waiting time for elderly patients in need of hip- or knee-replacement surgery is between 300 and 400 days. Some people in New Zealand waited for *two years* for their surgeries.[3]

An investigation by a British newspaper found that delays in treatment for colon cancer patients were so long that 20 percent of the cases were incurable by the time they finally received "treatment." The same was true of lung cancer patients; and 25 percent of British cardiac patients die waiting for treatment.[4]

Not surprisingly, those who can afford it seek treatment in other countries, like the United States. This is especially true of Canadians. Those who cannot afford it are simply out of luck. This despite the fact that healthcare socialism is always sold politically as a program to help "the poor" under the mindless slogan of "Healthcare for All."

Many British, Canadian, and other victims of healthcare socialism *die* waiting in line for what in the U.S. would be quick and routine medical treatment. In Canada, a young, eighteen-year-old girl named Laura Hillier died while waiting for a bone marrow transplant. An Ontario hospital claimed that it had thirty people waiting for the treatment but could only afford to perform five per month.[5] "Healthcare for All" obviously doesn't include people like Laura Hillier and thousands of others each year just like her.

The United States is not completely immune from shortages thanks to socialist Medicaid and Medicare and the heavy regulation of the healthcare system. For example, doctors believe that hundreds of thousands of people on kidney dialysis would benefit from six-day-a-week treatment, but Medicare only covers three days because of "global budget controls." Similar shortages occur in many other Medicare- or Medic-aid-funded areas; "free" colonoscopies have led to shortages where in some parts of the United States patients must wait for months.[6]

But if one conducts an Internet search of "hospital shortages in Canada," one discovers that the Canadian government is constantly issuing warnings to the public about nursing shortages,[7] drug shortages,[8] hospital bed shortages,[9] medicine shortages,[10] and doctor shortages.[11] Hospital bed shortages become so acute at times that hospital administrators resort to cancelling surgeries; allowing patients to languish on stretchers in cold, dirty, disease-infected hallways; and discharging them before they should, simply to make room for other patients. Such conditions have led to numerous outbreaks of infectious diseases in Canadian hospitals.[12]

Advocates of "single-payer healthcare" (single-payer means the taxpayer) in the American media rarely reveal the horrors of such a system in other countries, but every once in a while the truth slips out. One example is a January 16, 2000, *New York Times* article by James Brooke entitled "Full Hospitals Make Canadians Wait and Look South." The article revealed very interesting information about price control-induced shortages in Canada: a fifty-eight-year-old grandmother on a *five-year* waiting list for heart surgery awaited open-heart surgery in a Montreal hospital hallway with sixty-six other patients as electric doors opened and closed all night long, bringing in drafts from below-zero weather; twenty-three of Toronto's twenty-five hospitals turned away ambulances in a single day because of a doctor shortage; Vancouver ambulances were "stacked up for hours" while heart attack victims waited in them; and at least 1,000 Canadian doctors had recently migrated to the United States to avoid price controls on their salaries. "Few Canadians would recommend their system as a model for export," Mr. Brooke concluded.[13]

Contrary to the "Healthcare for All" rhetoric of the advocates of healthcare socialism, in the real world socialized healthcare is grossly inequitable because of the realities of politics and government. Whenever government allocates resources—for healthcare or anything else—the more affluent in society will always receive a disproportionate share of the benefits at the expense of the less affluent. As Friedrich Hayek once said, under socialism the only power worth having is political power, and the affluent are always better at wielding political power than are the poor.

As *The Guardian*, a British newspaper, concluded after researching the allocation of healthcare services by the British National Health Service: "Generally speaking, the poorer you are and the more socially deprived your area, the worse your care and access [to healthcare] is likely to be."[14] A British publication called *The Good Hospital Guide* found great disparities in access to healthcare, with the best-performing hospitals "near the wealthiest sectors of the city," whereas the hospitals with the worst performance "are located in east London, the most economically depressed area of the city."[15] The *Guide* found that hospitals in wealthier parts of the city had four times the number of doctors per one hundred patients as were found in the poorest parts of the city. Even more extreme inequalities in healthcare provision are found in the Canadian version of healthcare socialism. Spending on medical specialists was found in one study to be four times higher in affluent Vancouver than in poorer areas; per capita spending was three times higher in general; and residents of Vancouver benefited by as much as a thirty-to-one difference in the number of certain medical specialists available compared to poorer parts of British Columbia.[16]

Government rationing of medical technology is pervasive in countries with "single-payer," socialized healthcare. On a per capita basis, the United States has more than three times as many MRI units as Canada does; twice as many CT scanners; and much of the medical technology that does exist in Canada is archaic and obsolete compared to American medical technology.[17]

Socialist healthcare rationing can be especially bad for older patients, because they are seen as drags on the system. In Britain, for instance, even though one-third of all diagnosed cancers are in patients seventy-five years old or older, the British National Health Service does not provide cancer screening to those over sixty-five; and only one in fifty lung cancer patients over seventy-five receives surgery.[18] Some commentators have charged the British National Health Service with practicing "euthanasia." Even if euthanasia was not the *intent* of the British government, it has been the *effect* of healthcare socialism in that country. In Sweden, the government actually instructed doctors to "prioritize" patients according to their status as future taxpayers. The elderly are at the bottom of that list, since they are mostly retired and paying relatively little in taxes but receiving a relatively large share of government services.[19]

Just as America embarks on the road to healthcare socialism with the adoption of "Obamacare," most

European countries with socialized medicine are moving away from it by introducing market-oriented reforms that introduce a larger degree of private-sector competition in healthcare industries. In England more than seven million people have private health insurance and the British National Health Service is treating patients in private hospitals. There is now almost as much private-sector healthcare in Australia as in the United States as a percentage of all healthcare; Sweden allows private healthcare providers to supply almost half of all healthcare services and allows private health insurance; and the Canadian government spends more than $1 billion per year on healthcare services for Canadians delivered by American healthcare providers.[20] Thousands of Canadians essentially take healthcare "privatization" into their own hands each year by traveling to the United States for care.

THE FOUNDING FATHERS OF HEALTHCARE SOCIALISM

The Soviet Union was the first country to promise "cradle-to-grave," government-run healthcare coverage with all the same rhetoric that politicians in democratic countries now use: "the right to health," "healthcare for all," and all the rest of the clichés. Economist Yuri Maltsev, a professor at Carthage College in Wisconsin who was once an economic advisor to Mikhail Gorbachev, wrote that after decades of "fine tuning" healthcare socialism, "healthcare institutions in Russia were at least a hundred years behind the average U.S. level."[21] He described Russian hospitals during the peak of Russian socialism as characterized by "filth, odors, cats roaming the halls, drunken medical personnel, and absence of soap and cleaning supplies...."[22] Even the Russian government admitted that almost 80 percent of AIDS patients contracted the disease through dirty needles or HIV-tainted blood from the state-run hospitals.

Neurosurgeons were paid about one-third of what bus drivers were paid, said Professor Maltsev, which would not exactly attract the best and brightest to medical education. Patients had to pay bribes to be treated. Unscrupulous doctors solicited bribes by refusing to use anesthesia unless the patient paid up. In order to "improve" statistics about hospital deaths, "patients were routinely shoved out the door just before taking their last breath." The Russian system of healthcare socialism was characterized by "criminal negligence, bribes taken by medical apparatchiks, drunken ambulance crews, and food poisoning in hospitals and child-care facilities," said Maltsev.[23] After years of healthcare socialism, 57 percent of all Russian hospitals did not even have running hot water, and 36 percent of hospitals in rural areas did not have water or sewage treatment at all.[24]

For example, Maltsev recalled "the case of a four-teen-year-old girl from my district [he was a "People's Deputy" in Moscow from 1987-1989] who died of acute nephritis in a Moscow hospital. She died because a doctor decided that it was better to save 'precious' X-ray film (imported by the Soviets for hard currency) instead of double-checking his diagnosis.... Instead, the doctor treated the teenager with a heat compress, which killed her almost instantly."[25] To make matters worse, "There was no legal remedy for the girl's parents and grandparents. By definition, a single-payer system cannot allow any such remedy.... The doctor received no official reprimand."[26]

The Soviet Union, like all socialist countries, had a multi-tiered system where the political ruling class was exempted from the squalor of the hospitals that catered to the masses. They had special hospitals, special rooms, and all the medicine in the world reserved *for themselves*. As George Orwell might have said, with socialism all men are created equal, only some are more equal than others. Who in his right mind would want to emulate such a system except for the ruling political class that intends to exempt itself from all the squalor and horrors of socialized medicine?

There is nothing about all of this that was unique to the Soviet Union, Maltsev concluded. "It is a direct result of the government monopoly on healthcare and it can happen in any country.... Socialized medical systems have not served to raise general health or living standards anywhere. In fact, both analytical reasoning and empirical evidence point to the opposite conclusion. But the dismal failure of socialized medicine to raise people's health and longevity has not affected its appeal for politicians, administrators, and their intellectual servants in search of absolute power and control."[27]

10

HOW SOCIALISM
CAUSES POLLUTION

I n 1912 a British economist named Arthur C. Pigou
published a book entitled *Wealth and Welfare* in
which he explained what, ever since then, has been
the standard theory of the root causes of pollution and
other forms of environmental degradation.[1] Pigou
blamed pollution on the unregulated pursuit of profit
in a capitalistic economy where business people were
said to have incentives to consider the private costs of
their decisions (wages paid to employees, the cost of
raw materials, taxes, and so on), but not the "external"
or "social" costs such as the pollution that may harm
the environment or even public health. Consequently,

said Pigou, business people will largely ignore these "social costs" unless government steps in and forces them to pay for them. He then advocated pollution taxes in the form of a per-unit tax on production (such as a tax on every ton of steel manufactured in a steel mill or every ton of coal burned in a power plant). These taxes came to be known as "Pigouvian taxes" and have been advocated by most economists ever since as a possible means of alleviating pollution problems by forcing businesses to cut back on production under the understanding that anything that is taxed, we get less of.

At the same time, Pigou argued that such problems would never exist to any noticeable extent in a socialist economy, for a socialist "planning board" would always be wise and benevolent enough to take the external costs of pollution into account. He was wrong on both counts: businesses are not necessarily prone to pollute if there is a sound legal system that holds them liable for any damages that they may impose on others, and actual socialism during the twentieth century created an environmental nightmare.

HOW CAPITALISM PROTECTS THE ENVIRONMENT

One of the defining characteristics of capitalism—arguably the most important one—is the existence of private property and the protection of property rights. Just as important, property ownership involves *liability* for the use of one's property. Property owners realize the benefits of ownership, and are also responsible for any costs that their property imposes on others. Ownership of an automobile, for example, makes one *responsible* for any damages one may cause by crashing one's automobile into someone else's—as long as there exists a sound legal system that protects people's rights. Such a legal system existed in America for many years, until it was transformed in the late nineteenth century, as explained by legal scholar Morton J. Horwitz in his two-volume treatise, *The Transformation of American Law*.[2] Horwitz showed that up until the latter part of the nineteenth century, the common law regarding pollution was such that if a factory owner polluted a stream or the air in a way that caused financial, physical, and/or psychic harm to his neighbors, it was almost certain that he would be sued for damages by either individuals or communities, and would be found guilty. He would then be assessed a penalty. Economists call this "internalizing" the external costs of pollution. Pollution doesn't pay if polluters are held legally responsible for the damages caused by their polluting behavior.

The legal system changed, however, once the legal profession began to adopt a more collectivist, as opposed to an individualist, philosophy, as Horwitz explains. The individualist view is that the government's legal system should be based, first and foremost, on the protection of life, liberty, and property, including protection from pollution. The collectivist viewpoint that was adopted by the American legal profession argued the following: no individual or group of individuals should stand in the way of the economic progress of the entire community. Therefore, a few victims of pollution should not interfere with economic development prospects that benefit "the greater good." It was an application of the old utilitarian line, later adopted by the socialists, about "the greatest good for the greatest number." Polluters were increasingly let off the hook because of this collectivist corruption of the American legal system.

Competitive businesses in a capitalist economy actually have strong incentives to conserve and protect natural resources. Profit maximization—the main goal of any business—is after all the flip side of cost minimization. And a good way to minimize cost (and maximize profit) is to use as few resources as possible in producing goods or services in the marketplace. Coca-Cola, for example, found that by using less aluminum in its drink cans it could cut costs while maintaining quality, so it did. Whether it's a corporation looking to cut energy costs by conserving energy; an agribusiness, like forestry, that has an interest in keeping a renewable resource going; a smoke-stack industry that wants to maintain good relations with its neighbors and customers; or even a simple homeowner who has a natural motivation to maintain and improve the value of his lot, a sort of (Adam) Smithian invisible environmental hand guides private ownership and free-market businesses.[3] If you've ever noticed how car owners treat their property compared to how rental cars get treated, or how homeowners treat their homes and property compared to how renters treat theirs, you'll understand the point.

Renters, though, can at least be held accountable by the property owner or the rent-a-car company. Land socialism takes irresponsibility a big step further. Timber companies, for example, that operate their own forests are extremely careful about being good stewards of their land, because it is their livelihood; they even innovate with the creation and planting of "super trees" that mature more quickly than normal trees. The practice of "clear-cutting" forests, as well as overgrazing cattle and the resulting desertification in parts of the West, was the direct result, in most cases, of timber companies operating, or cattle ranchers grazing their herds, on government-owned land. Because they didn't own the land, they had little direct incentive to care for it; that was the government's responsibility, and the government was often too slow to react.[4]

SOCIALISM'S ENVIRONMENTAL NIGHTMARES

The environmental perils of government ownership are even more pronounced under socialism. The collapse of the Soviet empire in the late 1980s and early 1990s provided a glimpse, for the first time in decades, of the environmental conditions in such closed societies as socialist Russia, East Germany, Poland, Czechoslovakia, and elsewhere. What emerged was a tragic story of grotesque environmental destruction.

Small groups can use property communally, and through the threat of fines and social ostracism, make it work—the sort of thing you see in homeowner associations and community clubhouses. But when property is owned communally on a large scale or by the government and treated as a free resource, it will inevitably be abused because no one has either the motivation of profit or even the simple pride of ownership to care for and maintain the land for future profit or future generations; it is simply something to be used *now*. In the Soviet Union, such socialist attitudes and policies led to an environmental scandal of epic proportions exposed in books like *Ecocide in the USSR*.[5] A typical example comes from the Soviet Union's exploitation of the Black Sea.[6] To meet government-issued five-year plans for housing and other construction, builders extracted gravel and sand from around

Black Sea beaches (and knocked down a lot trees to do so). Because there was no private property, no value was attached to the gravel, or to the trees, or to the shoreline. Because the gravel was "free," contractors hauled away as much as possible—before someone else did. The result, of course, was massive erosion of the beach. Between 1920 and 1960, the Black Sea coastline shrank by half, the area was scarred by hundreds of landslides every year, and hotels, hospitals, and a military sanitarium collapsed into the sea as the shoreline gave way.

For similar reasons—a lack of private ownership, no commercial incentive to be good environmental stewards, the stifling of economic and technical progress that comes with socialism—water pollution was catastrophic in socialist Russia. The West has had its fair share of environmental problems, including river pollution, but nothing like what went on behind the Iron Curtain. Effluent from a chemical plant killed almost all the fish in the Oka River in 1965, and similar fish kills occurred in the Volga, Ob, Yenesi, Ural, and Northern Divina Rivers. Most Russian factories discharged their waste without cleaning it at all. Mines, oil wells, and ships freely dumped waste and ballast into any available body of water. Only six of the twenty main cities in Moldavia had a sewer system by the late 1960s, and only two of those cities were successful in actually treating sewage. Conditions were far more primitive—and polluted—in the countryside.

The Aral and Caspian seas had been slowly disappearing during the socialist era as huge quantities of their water were diverted for irrigation. Since untreated sewage flowed into their feeder rivers, they were heavily polluted as well. Near the end of the socialist era in Russia, some government authorities there predicted that by the end of the century the Aral Sea would essentially become a salt marsh. Because of the rising salt content fish had been disappearing, and the sea itself had shrunk by about one-third. Its shoreline was described as "an arid desert" where the wind blew dry deposits of salt thousands of miles away. The infant mortality rate in that area was five times the national average.[7]

The sturgeon population was so devastated in the Caspian Sea from overfishing and pollution that the Soviets actually experimented with producing "artificial caviar." Hundreds of socialist factories and oil refineries and the major cities along the Caspian Sea dumped untreated waste and sewage into it. The concentration of oil in the Volga River was so great that steamboats were equipped with signs forbidding passengers to toss cigarettes overboard for fear that the river might catch fire. Fish kills along the Volga River were a common occurrence.

Lake Baikal, which is one of the largest and deepest freshwater lakes in the world, was horribly polluted. Factories and pulp mills dumped hundreds of millions of gallons of poisonous effluent into the lake for decades. As a result, animal life in the lake was reduced by half; untreated sewage was dumped into all the tributaries to the lake. Islands of alkaline sewage were observed floating in Lake Baikal, including one that was eighteen miles long and three miles wide. These "islands" polluted the air around the lake as well as the lake itself. Because no one owned it and had any interest in preserving it, thousands of acres of forest land around the lake were denuded, causing dust storms.[8] Most of this horrible environmental degradation occurred because of the socialist government's goal of pursuing "economic growth" at any cost.

Communist China has followed socialist Russia down a path of environmental destruction. According to the Worldwatch Institute, by the early 1990s more than 90 percent of the trees in the pine forests of China's Sichuan province had died from air pollution. In Chungking, the largest city in southwest China, a 4,500-acre forest was reduced in half by pollution, and acid rain was reported to have caused massive crop destruction. Depletion of government-owned forest land had resulted in desertification, and millions of acres of grazing land in the Northern Chinese plains were made alkaline and unproductive. China's environmental problems are not just rural. CBS News reported in 2007 that sixteen of the world's twenty most polluted cities were in China.[9]

Throughout the Communist world, environmental conditions were horrendous. The Polish Academy of Sciences reported in the early 1990s that a third of the country's thirty-eight million people had lived in areas of "ecological disaster." In the heavily industrialized Katowice region of Poland, the people suffered from 15 percent more circulatory disease; 30 percent more tumors; and 47 percent more respiratory disease than did other Poles. Acid rain was reported to have so corroded railroad tracks in socialist Poland that trains were not allowed to exceed twenty- four miles an hour. The air was so polluted in Katowice that there were underground "clinics" for those with chronic lung diseases. These took place in uranium mines where there was supposedly clean air.[10]

Non-stop pumping of water from coal mines caused so much land to subside that more than 300,000 apartments were destroyed as high-rise buildings collapsed into sinkholes. Mine sludge pumped into rivers and streams, along with untreated sewage, made 95 percent of the water in socialist Poland unfit for human consumption. More than 65 percent of the nation's water was unfit even for industrial use. It was so toxic that it would destroy heavy metals used by industry. Acid rain dissolved so much of the gold roof of the sixteenth-century Sigismund Chapel that it had to be replaced.[11]

In socialist Poland industrial dust containing poisonous substances such as cadmium, lead, zinc, and iron rained down on the cities. Trucks would drive through the streets daily spraying water to reduce the poisonous dust. The largest river in Poland—the Vistula —was described by the mayor of Krakow as a "sewage canal." Half of Poland's cities did not even treat their wastes; dozens of animal species became extinct; and health problems among children were epidemic in the industrial regions. Life expectancy for men *fell* in socialist Poland while it was rising substantially in much of the rest of the world, especially the capitalist West.[12]

The then-Czechoslovakian President Vaclav Havel announced in 1990 that his country had the worst environment in all of Europe, thanks to forty-five years of socialism. He wasn't exaggerating. Sulfur dioxide concentrations were reported to be eight times higher than in the United States. Because of decades of chemical fertilizer overuse, farmland in some parts of Czechoslovakia was toxic to more than a foot in depth. In Bohemia, hills were barren because pollution had killed all the vegetation. The air was so foul that it was said it could be tasted. Hundreds of thousands of acres of forests disappeared due to pollution; a thick, brown haze is reported to have hung over much of northern Czechoslovakia for most of the year; aluminum had poisoned the ground water in vast areas of the country; in its search for coal the socialist government used bulldozers on such a massive scale that it turned what had been towns, farms, and woodlands into wastelands.

In East Germany in the late 1980s, 80 percent of the surface waters were unsuitable for fishing, swimming, or drinking, and one-third of all lakes had been declared biologically dead because of untreated sewage that had been dumped into them for decades. One-fifth of all forests were dead, the victims of pollution, with many more slowly dying. The air was so polluted in some cities that cars used their headlights all day long; and visitors were known to vomit upon breathing the air. [13] Nearly identical spectacles occurred in Bulgaria, Romania, and Yugoslavia during the socialist era.

"DEMOCRATIC" SOCIALIST POLLUTION

Socialism does not have to be totalitarian to produce environmental nightmares. Socialism is socialism. Government-run enterprises are just as inept

under democratic governments as they are under auto-
cratic governments. One egregious example of environmental degradation in a democratic socialist
country is Venezuela, thanks to its nationalized oil
industry and lack of private property rights over much
its natural resources. Venezuela suffers from massive
deforestation, losing forest at twice the rate of other
South American countries.[14] Lake Maracaibo is heavily polluted with industrial wastes that include mer-
cury and other deadly substances; 10,000 gallons of
sewage *per second* is dumped into the lake from the
two million people who live around the lake; more
than 800 companies are permitted to dump industrial
waste into the lake; and there are frequent oil spills,
sometimes more than one a day.[15]

The equally enormous Valencia Lake is said to be
"massively polluted due to the countless sewage systems" that pour into it.[16] The city of Valencia gets
its water supply from the Pao-Cachinche dam, and the
water held by the dam receives about 80 percent of
the sewage from Valencia. The water treatment facilities are said to be often "in disrepair."[17] In 2007, the
Venezuelan government decided to pump water that it
knew was unfit for human consumption from Valencia
Lake into the Pao-Cachinche dam. Meanwhile, the
government-run oil company, known by the acronym
PDVSA, had by the late 1990s filled some 15,000 oil

pits with contaminated sludge from oil wells. All of this is bound to seep into the groundwater, creating serious health threats.

It is a hallmark of socialist governments everywhere to nationalize heavy industries like petroleum, and, in the process, turn them into government-supervised environmental criminals unaccountable to property owners and consumers. For example, when privately owned British Petroleum (BP) caused an accidental oil spill in the Gulf of Mexico, it immediately established a $20 billion fund to pay future claims of damages and did everything it could to clean up the mess. It had legal obligations and its corporate reputation at stake. When the Mexican government's oil company, Pemex, causes an oil spill in the Gulf of Mexico—and there have been many—it claims "sovereign immunity" from any legal damages. In the first five months of 2015, Pemex was responsible for three catastrophic oil rig explosions in the Gulf of Mexico that caused several deaths, numerous injuries to oil platform workers, and generated air and water pollution.[18] Pemex claimed that the explosions caused no oil spill, but satellite images taken by Greenpeace Mexico showed a two-and-a-half-mile long oil slick reaching from the exploded oil platform.[19] "Pemex has proven time and time again that you cannot trust their statements," said Gustavo Ampugnani of Greenpeace Mexico.[20]

The United States is not immune from socialist-driven environmental problems. Many utility companies, for example, are government-owned with less than stellar results. In 2015, to take just one recent example, the people of Flint, Michigan, were alerted to a frightening environmental debacle. The city government, supposedly in an effort to save money, switched its city's water supply from Lake Huron to the Flint River, despite the fact that the Flint River had long been known to be extraordinarily polluted. The Flint city government (and the state's Department of Environmental Quality, according to a class action lawsuit) failed to properly treat water from the Flint River. The result was that city residents drank and bathed in water full of lead and other dangerous chemicals. [21]

For many intellectuals, the attraction of socialism is that it is "rational"; it is a "planned" economy, planned by people like them. In reality, the environmental and economic results of socialism are a litany of disaster.

11

KARL MARX'S "PROGRESSIVE" INCOME TAX

A "heavy progressive or graduated income tax" was the second most important priority of Karl Marx, the godfather of totalitarian communism. It was the second plank of the ten-plank policy platform in *The Communist Manifesto*. The first plank was "Abolition of property in land...." All ten planks were designed as a means of undermining and destroying private enterprise in capitalist countries to pave the way for socialism.

One reason why Marx and other socialists advocated (and advocate) a discriminatory income tax that penalizes productivity by taxing higher incomes at progressively higher tax rates is their denial of the reality of human inequality. In a capitalist economy, those who are more skilled at serving their fellow man by providing him with valued goods and services will earn higher incomes than those with fewer skills. No two human beings are ever "equal" in that regard. The ideal of a "progressive" income tax is to create greater "equality" by treating people unequally. It is the exact opposite of the fundamental principal of fairness in a free society, which is equality *under the law.* A progressive income tax is a policy of *inequality* under the law. If you're a socialist, exploiting envy is a great way to destabilize a capitalist society.

Another reason why socialists advocate for a progressive income tax is because Marxists believe the "working class" is forever being "exploited" by capitalist bosses. Punishing capitalists and high wage earners by taxing them at discriminatory rates would, in theory, fund a welfare state for "the workers"—or often for those who preferred not to work.

Another economic reality that progressive taxation ignores is what economists call "human capital development." In a capitalist economy, workers who improve their skills and productivity are rewarded with higher wages, because employers will compete for their services. This is why, in a capitalist economy, people hone their work skills, continue their education, develop good work habits, and become more productive in general, because productivity is rewarded.

Capitalism *encourages* upward mobility. It is socialism and welfare that keeps the "working class," or the nonworking class, stuck at subsistence level wages or benefits. In the twentieth century, nearly everyone in the Soviet Union or socialist Eastern Europe lived in poverty by western standards, while the socialist ruling elite enjoyed lives of privilege. As usual, Marx got it backwards: capitalism is the driving force of economic advancement for the working class; socialism impoverishes the working class.

In capitalist economies the "distribution" of income tends to be diamond shaped, with a few billionaires at the top and a few poor people at the bottom. Because that's where the money is for a tax-hungry government, a "progressive" income tax is inevitably a discriminatory *tax on the aspiring middle class*, punishing people who have advanced economically through their own hard work, education, and perseverance.

THE ENGINE OF
CLASS WARFARE

Hardly any aspect of government creates more conflict and acrimony than the income tax. The table below—based on IRS data from 2012—shows how the income tax burden falls in the United States. About 45 percent of all Americans at the lower-income levels pay *no* income tax at all, while the top half of income earners paid 97.2 percent of all income taxes collected.

WHO PAYS THE INCOME TAX, BY INCOME CATEGORY

Top 1%	Top 5%	Top 10%	Top 25%	Top 50%	Bottom 50%
38.1	58.9	70.2	86.4	97.2	2.8%

Source: IRS

There are two beneficiaries of the progressive income tax—those that receive more in government benefits than they pay in taxes (though how "beneficial" it is to live off welfare is debatable to say the least) and the government bureaucratic class that gets to distribute all the taxes collected. The losers are taxpayers and frankly, society at large, which would benefit if more government workers and welfare recipients actually engaged in free market businesses, commerce, and employment providing competitive goods and services that people want to buy of their own free will, which is how material progress is really made.

The progressive income tax also is an engine for destroying constitutional liberty, as the mid-nineteenth-century American statesman John C. Calhoun warned us. In his 1850 *Disquisition on Government,* Calhoun warned that a written constitution alone would not be sufficient to counteract "the tendency of the numerical majority to oppression and the abuse of power."[1] The "major and dominant party," if it represented the tax-consuming class, would work diligently, he said, to abolish constitutional restrictions on government authority. Calhoun predicted that, in time, the "party in favor of [constitutional] restrictions "would be over-powered" so that there would be no restraints on government spending. Constitutional restrictions on the powers of the state "would ultimately be annulled," Calhoun wrote, "and the government converted into one of unlimited powers."[2] Many would say he was prescient.

THE "ESSENCE OF SOCIALISM"

It was hardly an accident that "a heavy progressive or graduated income tax" was the second plank of *The Communist Manifesto* next to the "abolition of property," for the two go hand in hand. Income taxes in general, and especially progressive income taxes, are "a denial of private property," wrote Frank Chodorov in *The Income Tax: Root of All Evil.*[3] Governments that impose an income tax, wrote Chodorov, tell their citizens: "Your earnings are not exclusively your own; we have a claim on them, and our claim precedes yours; we will allow you to keep some of it, because we recognize your need, not your right; but whatever we grant you for yourself is for us to decide."[4] When the government decides what percentage of your income you can keep, your income, which is your property, has been socialized; and if you don't agree with "the needs of government," you can face a long prison sentence. In theory, there is no limit to the amount of income that can be confiscated through taxation. The original income tax, ratified by the Sixteenth Amendment to the Constitution in 1913, had a top marginal rate of 7 percent at an income threshold of $500,000. By 1918, the top rate of taxation had risen to 77 percent; then to 88 percent in 1944; and 91 percent from 1950 to 1963. The top rate was reduced by the Kennedy Tax Cuts in the early 1960s, but was still 70 percent in 1980 on the eve of the Reagan Tax Cuts, which eventually dropped the top rate to 28 percent.

When the progressive income tax was adopted in 1913, "the absolute right of property in the United States was violated," wrote Chodorov.[5] And "that, of course, is the essence of socialism. Whatever else socialism is, or is claimed to be, its first tenet is the denial of private property."[6] This is why "all socialists, beginning with Karl Marx, have advocated income taxation, the heavier the better."[7] And of course Marx was an adamant advocate of a "heavy" *progressive* income tax because of another dictum of *The Communist Manifesto*—that tax policy should be guided by the admonition, "from each according to his ability, to each according to his need." The more "able" you are, the heavier should be the burden of income tax confiscation.

This may sound appealing to the envious who want to plunder "the rich," but the fact remains that it is the *middle class* that, collectively, has the biggest "ability to pay" because it earns most of the income in any capitalistic society. That is why political demagogues who use "soak the rich" rhetoric are often revealed to believe that the "rich" includes just about anyone who earns a lower-middle-class income or higher.

For a portion of the year, those who pay income taxes are essentially slaves to the state, while those who receive more "benefits" than they pay in taxes are wards of the state all year long. Either way, the government wins, and the taxpayers and the economy and individual freedom are the losers.

MONOPOLY GOVERNMENT

Socialists believe in vesting as much power in the central government as possible in order to have a government-planned society, with a single plan imposed on the entire nation. Socialized healthcare, for example, forces everyone to receive the same healthcare *as defined by the state.*

More decentralized government, by contrast, means more *competitive* government, where citizens can adopt policies that deviate from the One Socialist Plan. Decentralized, competitive government is the essence of American federalism created by the founding fathers. Socialists denigrate American federalism as reactionary, as the excuse for states' rights that were invoked to defend slavery, Jim Crow laws, and every other conceivable sin ever committed by state and local governments, while ignoring federalism's crucial role, which the founders understood, in preserving freedom. Frank Chodorov pinpointed the importance of decentralized government to a free society when he wrote:

> The real obstacle [to tyranny] is the psychological resistance to centralization that the States' rights tradition fosters. The citizen of divided allegiance cannot be reduced to subservience; if he is in the habit of serving two political gods he cannot be dominated by either one.... No political authority ever achieved absolutism until the people were deprived of a choice of loyalties.[8]

It was no accident that Stalin, Mussolini, Hitler, and Lenin liquidated all competing authorities, including the clergy. Government "cannot give [us] freedom," Chodorov continued; "it can only take it away. The more power the government exercises the less freedom will the people enjoy. And when government has a monopoly of power the people have no freedom. This is the definition of absolutism—monopoly of power."[9] Moreover, it is the progressive income tax that "has made of the United States as completely centralized a nation as any that went before it, the very kind of establishment the Founding Fathers abhorred...."[10]

Chodorov wrote that in 1954; American government has become even vastly more centralized since then. How this happened is as follows:

> [B]y enabling the federal government to put its hands into the pockets and pay envelopes of the people, [the progressive income tax] drew their allegiance away from their local governments. It made them citizens of the United States rather than of their respective states. Their loyalty followed their money, which was now taken from them not by their local representatives, over whom they had some control, but by the

> representatives of the other...states. They
> became subject to the will of the central
> government.[11]

The state and local governments have also become more-or-less franchises of the federal government, which can easily bribe or threaten them into submission with promises of federal grants or of their denial.

Chodorov was certainly not the only one to recognize the importance of decentralized government in preserving a free and prosperous society. The founding fathers certainly did, as did some of the most brilliant defenders of freedom in modern times. In his book *Omnipotent Government*, Ludwig von Mises wrote that with the growth of Big Government around the world:

> New powers accrued not to the member
> states but to the federal government. Every
> step toward more government interference
> and more planning means at the same time
> an expansion of the jurisdiction of the central
> government. Washington and Berne
> [Switzerland] were once the seats of the
> federal governments; today they are capitals
> in the true sense of the word, and the
> states and cantons are virtually reduced to

the status of provinces. It is a very significant fact that the adversaries of the trend toward more government controls describe their opposition as a fight against Washington and against Berne, i.e., against centralization. It is conceived as a contest of states' rights versus the central power.[12]

Felix Morley, author of *Freedom and Federalism*, wrote that "Socialism and federalism are necessarily political opposites because the former demands that centralized concentration of power which the latter by definition denies."[13]

In contrast, all of the worst tyrants in world history were impassioned enemies of decentralized political power. Adolf Hitler himself devoted an entire chapter of *Mein Kampf* to a vitriolic denunciation of federalism and states' rights in Germany. Hitler denounced the alleged "fragmentation" and "impotence" of the "so-called sovereign states" and praised his predecessors for all but abolishing state sovereignty or states' rights in Germany.[14] He considered this to be a great victory in what he called the "struggle between federalism and centralization."[15]

Blaming the idea of federalism on "the Jews" (naturally), Hitler declared that his "National Socialists…would totally eliminate states' rights altogether."[16]

As with all socialists, national, international, or whatever, Hitler promised that "National Socialism…must lay claim to the right to force its principles on the whole German nation without consideration of previous federated state boundaries…."[17] This of course is the essence of socialism: the forceful imposition of one government "plan" or plans on a whole society.

ECONOMIC CHAOS

There is nothing inherently "fair" or equitable about how the funds raised by a progressive income tax are spent. The pattern of government expenditures will be determined by the laws of politics. That is, they will go to the most politically influential. This rarely includes the poor in whose name progressive taxation is always sold. In fact, most government income redistribution takes place within the middle class: middle-class taxpayers pay for government subsidies to middle-class farmers, college students, and school teachers and other government employees.[18]

There are also many government programs that tax middle-income taxpayers to provide subsidies for the affluent and the wealthy. Government bailouts of Wall Street investment banks, Export-Import Bank subsidies, farm subsidies to large agricultural corporations, and corporate welfare of all kinds would be examples of this.[19]

Nor is "fairness" achieved by imposing high income taxes on "erratic earners," like the novelist who struggles for years and then is punished with punitive income taxes when she finally becomes a bestseller; or the entrepreneur living on the verge of bankruptcy trying to build a business before finally succeeding. It seems perverse, to say the least, to punish such hard-earned success, especially when, in the case of the entrepreneur, he could use the income earned by his success to reinvest in his business and create new jobs and products, instead of financing more government bureaucracy and giving politicians more money for income-transfer programs.

Economists know that the progressive income tax encourages some of the most creative and productive people in society not to work. For example, in the late 1970s, a professional couple (married architects, for example) could earn enough income by early fall to push them into the 70 percent federal income tax bracket. That meant that for every additional $1000 they earned, they owed the federal government $700 (on top of any state and local income tax obligations). That was a powerful incentive for thousands of hard-working, higher-income earners to simply quit working and take a vacation as opposed to handing over most of their additional earnings to federal, state, and local governments. While long vacations might sound pleasant, the result was that jobs and wealth and products and services that could have been created were not because of government disincentives.

High earners always find ways around progressive income taxes, either by moving themselves or their money to lower-tax havens. Millions of man-hours are spent by lawyers and accountants trying to help their clients minimize their tax bills. One study found that after the state of Maryland adopted a special "millionaires' tax" in 2007, the state lost 31,000 high-income residents and $1.7 billion in tax revenue over the next three years, after which the "millionaires' tax" was ended.[20]

Frank Chodorov was not exaggerating when he wrote that many of the freedoms that Americans gained from the Revolution of 1776 were lost in the Revolution of 1913 with the adoption of the progressive income tax. The fact that the income tax has now been around for more than a hundred years is no reason to accept it and not push for its repeal.

12

MINIMUM WAGE, MAXIMUM FOLLY

Both the Socialist Party USA and Democratic Socialists of America highlight the idea of a super minimum wage law—a "living wage"—on their websites. The former group says that "the current left and progressive labor movement's call for a $15 minimum wage" is an important element of its "democratic socialist vision."[1] The latter group bemoans the existing minimum wage law as "basically criminal" and calls for its own version of a much higher minimum wage.[2]

The obvious question here is: Why do these socialists advocate a policy that is so stingy toward lower-wage workers? Why do they propose a fifteen dollar an hour "living wage" and not a $150 an hour "living-high-on-the-hog" wage? The Democratic Socialists of America say that even a twenty dollar an hour "living wage" would be "an unrealistic goal in our current political climate given the power of the right...."[3] Politics, they say, is the only thing holding them back. Otherwise, sure, a $150 an hour minimum wage would be a great thing.

Socialists routinely reject economic logic and reality, which tells us that minimum wage laws actually discriminate *against* relatively unskilled, entry-level workers, especially teenagers just getting started in the job market. Want to make it harder for new workers to get a job? Impose a minimum wage.

Socialists believe that low and unfair wages are inherent in the capitalist system because they adhere to the long-disproven Marxian "labor theory of value," which holds that labor is the sole source of value. From that perspective, employers essentially steal that value from workers. As the Democratic Socialists of America explain: "In a capitalist system working people will always fall short of justice when it comes to wages, since the basic logic of the system dictates that a small group of owners appropriates the wealth generated by a company, which then reluctantly forks over a small portion of that wealth to the workers who created it."[4]

One implication of this theory is that "social justice" is served by using the coercive powers of government to confiscate at least some of the allegedly ill-gotten profits of capitalists with minimum wage laws, corporation income taxes, nationalization of industry, and any other available means. The economy is viewed as a "zero-sum game"—that is, every dollar in the pocket of a capitalist is a dollar that was unjustly taken from the pocket of a worker.

THE ECONOMIC REALITY OF MINIMUM WAGE LAWS

Across time and across countries, economists know that minimum wage laws harm low-skilled workers. In 1979, a survey of American professional economists found that 90 percent agreed that higher minimum wages increase unemployment, especially for young and unskilled workers.[5] It simply prices them out of the job market, demanding more for their services than they are likely to produce for an employer in profit. In the twenty-first century, *New York Times* columnist Paul Krugman, in his widely read textbook on microeconomics (coauthored with Robin Wells), describes the effects of super-high minimum wage laws in such European countries as Greece and Spain. The "disproportionately young, from the ages of 18 to 30," are "locked out [of employment] without any prospect of finding a good job."[6] In these countries "a generation of young people is unable to get adequate job training, develop careers, and save for their future," thanks to high minimum wage laws.[7] "These young people," moreover, "are also more likely to engage in crime."[8]

In the 1930s, the original federal minimum wage law had a similar effect in poor communities in the United States. The minimum wage was set at twenty-five cents an hour, when the average American wage was 62.7 cents. Only about 300,000 workers in a labor force of fifty-four million were covered by the law.[9] But in Puerto Rico, where the average wage was only about twelve cents an hour, the effect of the minimum wage law was catastrophic; businesses could not afford to pay it. As reported by the *New York Times*: "[T]he law applied to Puerto Rico ends employment for approximately 120,000 persons. It is also believed to terminate prospects for any possible further industrialization."[10] The unemployment rate in Puerto Rico eventually approached 50 percent.

Another group disproportionately hit by the federal minimum wage law is black teenagers. All teenagers suffer from a higher unemployment rate, but since the advent of minimum wage laws in the 1930s, the black teenage unemployment rate has been as much as two-and-a-half times higher than the white teenage unemployment rate.[11] To pick just one year (2015), for example, while the "official" national unemployment rate, according to the U.S. Bureau of Labor Statistics, was 4.3 percent, the white teenage (sixteen to nineteen) unemployment rate was just under 14 percent while the black teenage unemployment rate was 23 percent.[12]

The reason is that teenagers, compared to the rest of the working population, are less well educated and skilled, and therefore less productive as employees. Minimum wage laws take away their one competitive advantage, which is price. In a free market, an employer might choose to hire a lower-priced, if less productive employee, and train her on the job. Minimum wage laws make that unaffordable for many employers; and black teenagers in lower-income neighborhoods, educated at dysfunctional and sometimes downright fraudulent public schools, are put at an even greater competitive disadvantage by minimum wage laws. Lower education levels translate into lower job skill levels in the eyes of employers. It's hard to get even an entry-level job if the government-run schools have failed to adequately teach basic reading, writing, math, and communication skills. That is why increases in the minimum wage are so disproportionately harmful to black inner-city teenagers.

LABOR UNIONS AND
THE MINIMUM WAGE

The Socialist Party USA proudly boasts that "progressive labor unions" are leading the way for a more than doubling of the federal minimum wage. Unions don't care about "the poor," they care about their members, and few of their members are minimum wage workers. Unions support increases in the minimum wage because they understand that low-skilled, non-union labor is often a substitute, in the eyes of employers, for more experienced, unionized labor. Their goal has always been to use the minimum wage law *against* labor market competition. They are happy to use groups like the Socialist Party USA and Democratic Socialists of America as dupes or pawns in their efforts to price the least-skilled and lowest-paid workers out of jobs.

Economist Walter Williams noted, for instance, that during the Apartheid era in South Africa, construction unions used minimum wage "equal pay" laws to eliminate the competitive advantage of black construction workers who were willing to work for $1.52 an hour less than white workers.[13] American labor unions have similarly pushed for minimum wage laws that take away the competitive advantage of less expensive, often ethnic minority, workers. In 1955, four American textile industry unions testified before Congress demanding an increase in the Puerto Rican minimum wage. They complained that the "wage gap" between Puerto Rican and American textile workers gave Puerto Rico "competitive advantages over the mainland."[14] Economist Simon Rottenberg pointed out that the unions' intention was "not to improve the conditions of Puerto Rican workers so much as to deprive those workers of employment opportunities by compelling them to offer their services at a high legally defined price.... The minimum wage law is an instrumental tactic employed by unions to achieve that purpose."[15]

It wasn't just Puerto Rico, it was the largely non-unionized American South, which, in the 1930s, was providing vigorous competition to northern industries. Northern unions, with the support of northern corporations, agitated for higher minimum wage laws to deny southern firms their competitive advantage.[16] As explained by Senator Paul Douglas (who was also a professional economist): "So far as the employers were concerned, the northern textile industry was definitely in favor of the bill [to raise the minimum wage], and opposed to the granting of any regional differentials. It welcomed a national scale as a means of protecting themselves against southern competition with lower wages."[17]

Massachusetts industrialists and politicians were especially vociferous in their push for a higher minimum wage that would hamstring southern industry with higher costs. The governor of Massachusetts, Charles Hurley, wrote a letter to members of Congress from his state stating how "important it is for such Federal legislation to be adopted" so that "Massachusetts [was] to have equal competition with other sections of the country," meaning of course the South.[18] Massachusetts protectionists in Congress bitterly complained that southern factories provided "corrosive competition."[19] In other words, southern factories were providing jobs for southern workers who were outcompeting their northern counterparts.

Labor unions and certain corporations have long collaborated to support higher minimum wage laws in order to price low-skilled, competing laborers out of jobs. At the same time, unions have also lobbied for government job-training programs, food stamps, and other forms of welfare for those who are thrown out of work by higher minimum wages. As Walter Williams explains: "[I]f unemployment [caused by higher minimum wages] meant starvation, there might be considerable political resistance to higher mandated wages. Unions therefore have incentives to support...income-subsidy programs, such as the Job Corps, the Comprehensive Training and Education Act, summer work programs, food stamps, public service employment, and welfare.... Income-subsidy programs disguise the true effects of labor market restrictions caused by unions...by casting a few crumbs to those denied jobs in order to keep them quiet, thereby contributing to the creation of a permanent welfare class."[20]

It is difficult to think of a quicker means of increasing poverty than adopting minimum wage laws, let alone "super" minimum wage laws. Minimum wage laws are a contributing factor to maximum unemployment.

13

HOW SOCIALIST REGULATION MAKES MONOPOLIES

Socialists long ago discovered that it wasn't always necessary to *own* the means of production; a system of pervasive government regulation can, in theory, be just as effective in *controlling* an economy but without the ordeal of actually confiscating—and figuring out how to operate—factories and other businesses. This was the brand of socialism known as fascism that was adopted in Italy and Germany in the early twentieth century. In leftist circles, fascism, though it no longer goes by that name, is making a comeback as progressivism and the regulatory state.

After the worldwide collapse of socialism in the Soviet Empire in the late 1980s and early 1990s, the American socialist economist Robert Heilbroner famously admitted in *The New Yorker* magazine (September 10, 1990) that "Mises was right" all along about the impossibility of a socialist economy. He did not, however, endorse capitalism and markets.[1] Quite the contrary: he concluded his essay by recommending that his fellow socialists turn to regulation—specifically, environmental regulation—as a means of centrally planning the U.S. economy under the guise of "saving the planet." Regulation, he said, could be just as effective as government ownership of the means of production.

For leftists, regulation is a gift that keeps on giving, because there is always another reason to increase the reach of the regulatory state—even to compensate for previous *failures* of the regulatory state, such as the Great Recession of 2008, which was a direct result of the policies of the Federal Reserve Board, the Federal National Mortgage Association (Fannie Mae), the Federal Home Loan Mortgage Corporation (Freddie Mac), and Congress. One can never, after all, regulate enough. Machiavellian socialists understand that capitalism can be strangled through regulation. The goal can be either deconstruction of a free-market society or simply making business owners subservient to bureaucrats.

Most socialists aren't so much Machiavellian as utopian. They have a vision of benevolent "public servants" who will regulate businesses "in the public interest." This is what is taught in the public schools and universities; it's called the "public interest theory of regulation."[2] It is a theory that has never been associated with reality.

REGULATION FOR THE REGULATED

The reality is that, historically, regulation is usually the result of lobbying by industry (and sometimes unions) to stifle or eliminate competition.

An early example of regulation-for-the-regulated is the "public utilities" industry. The standard story is that around the beginning of the twentieth century, water, electricity, natural gas, and telephone services were evolving into giant "natural" monopolies. In order to protect consumers from these monopolies, state and local governments stepped in and established a system of public utility regulation (or socialized the industries outright). Utility companies became "franchise monopolies." Government-run public-utility commissions would ensure the companies earned reasonable but not monopolistic profits. That's the standard story of public utility "natural monopolies." None of it is true.

Economist Harold Demsetz studied the history of the public utilities industries and found that, contrary to the folklore of "natural" monopolies in the free market, there was in fact very vigorous competition and no evolution toward monopoly. For example:

> Six electric light companies were organized in the one year of 1887 in New York City. Forty-five electric light enterprises had the legal right to operate in Chicago in 1907. Prior to 1895, Duluth, Minnesota, was served by five electric lighting companies, and Scranton, Pennsylvania, had four in 1906.... During the latter part of the nineteenth century, competition was the usual situation in the gas industry in this country. Before 1884, six companies were operating in New York City...competition was common and especially persistent in the telephone industry.... Baltimore, Chicago, Cleveland, Columbus, Detroit, Kansas City, Minneapolis, Philadelphia, Pittsburgh, and St. Louis, among other larger cities, had at least two telephone services in 1905.[3]

The real story of how the "public utilities" became government-sanctioned monopolies was told in 1936 by an economist named George T. Brown in his book, *The Gas Light Company of Baltimore*.[4] The history of the Gas Light Company of Baltimore is similar—even identical in many ways—to the history of dozens of other "public utility" companies. The company constantly struggled with new competitors all through the nineteenth century, from its founding in 1816. It competed, but it also lobbied the Maryland state legislature to deny corporate charters to its competitors. By 1880 there were three competing gas light companies in Baltimore, and they attempted to form a cartel by merging into one company, but their plans were foiled when "Thomas Alva Edison introduced electric light which threatened the existence of all gas companies," wrote Brown.[5]

When monopoly did appear, it was the result of government regulation, not "natural" free-market competition. In 1890 a bill was introduced into the Maryland legislature that called for granting the Consolidated Gas Company (the new name of the Gas Light Company of Baltimore) a twenty-five-year monopoly (the contract was renewable) in exchange for an annual payment to the city of $10,000 and 3 percent of the company's dividends.[6] "[T]he development of utility regulation in Maryland typified the experience of other states," wrote George T. Brown.[7] It was all a matter of corporations sharing monopoly profits with government.

Economist Horace M. Gray researched the history of the "public utility concept" and concluded that "the public utility status was to be the haven of refuge for all aspiring monopolists who found it too difficult, too costly, or too precarious to secure and maintain monopoly by private action alone."[8] Virtually every aspiring monopolist wanted the government to designate him as a "natural monopoly," said Gray. This included the radio, real estate, milk, airline, coal, oil, and agriculture industries, to mention just a few.

HOW FOR LINED THE POCKETS OF CRONY CAPITALISTS

Horace Gray also wrote that "the whole NRA experiment may be regarded as an effort by big business to secure legal sanction for its monopolistic practices."[9] NRA in this instance means the "National Recovery Act," the cornerstone of the first two-and-a-half years of Franklin D. Roosevelt's "New Deal." The NRA empowered the federal government to fix the prices of hundreds of manufactured goods and to establish "codes of fair competition." As a rule of thumb, whenever governments use the phrase "fair competition," just substitute the word "no" for "fair" and you will understand the true meaning of the phrase.

The antitrust laws prohibiting "combinations in restraint of trade" were abandoned as the Roosevelt administration dictated monopoly prices in more than 700 industries covering 95 percent of all industries in America.[10] As economist Robert Higgs explained, "Big businessmen dominated the writing and implementing of the [price code] documents...the codes...generally aimed to suppress competition in any form it might take."[11] This included minimum prices and mandatory advance notice of price changes.

Many of these same businessmen had tried for years to form private cartels that would squelch competition, but cartels often fall apart when members cheat; increasing their sales by cutting prices. If government, however, acts as a cartel enforcer, cheating can be eliminated, as it was with the NRA price codes, creating the perfect monopoly scheme—at least until the U.S. Supreme Court ruled the National Recovery Act to be unconstitutional in 1935.

The NRA not only set monopoly prices for corporations, it limited imports and put quotas on oil production, both of which drove up prices and increased corporate profits. To the Roosevelt administration, a competitive free market amounted to nothing more than "economic cannibalism." Businessmen were "industrial pirates,"[12] conservative businessmen were "social Neanderthals," and businessmen who tried to sell more by cutting prices were denigrated as "chiselers," "cutthroats," and, ironically, practitioners of "monopolistic price slashing." On the other hand, monopolistic conspiracies in restraint of trade were labeled as "cooperative" or "associational" activities.[13] Massive NRA rallies in favor of higher prices reminded one historian of "the chauvinistic extravaganzas staged by the Nazis in Germany."[14]

The Roosevelt administration was under the misapprehension that low prices had caused the Great Depression, when in fact the Great Depression had caused low prices and artificially raising prices only increased people's hardship.

Every economics textbook teaches that cartels and monopolies profit by restricting supply and raising prices. Restricting supply means fewer workers are needed, so unemployment goes up. NRA regulation actually made unemployment worse and helped prolong the Great Depression. UCLA economists Harold Cole and Lee Ohanian estimated that if the NRA had never existed, the Great Depression would have ended in 1936, instead of after World War II.[15]

FDR'S FEAR OF FLYING

In 1938 the federal government's Civil Aeronautics Board (CAB) began regulating prices, routes, admission of new airlines, and just about every other aspect of the airline industry. For the next forty years, the

CAB administered a monopolistic cartel that benefited corporate airlines rather than consumers.

The CAB severely restricted competition in the domestic airline industry by allowing *no* new airlines after 1938 when there were sixteen airline companies operating in the United States. Several airlines became defunct, so that by 1978 there were only ten remaining, operating under a monopolistic route-sharing scheme.[16] Because airlines could not compete on prices or on routes, both of which were set by the CAB, they competed in other ways, such as offering "free" alcohol and food. In response, the CAB began regulating the size of sandwiches that could be offered!

Government-enforced monopolies are very effective tools of corporate welfare. In 1974, it cost $1,442 to fly from New York to Los Angeles. In 1978, after the industry was finally deregulated, the same route cost $268. This is a typical example of how "regulation in the public interest" isn't.

Once the CAB monopoly was broken, the number of airlines increased; competition blossomed; and air fares plummeted. Airports themselves, however, are run by state and local governments; privatizing them would greatly reduce travel delays.

From 1935 until 1980 the trucking industry in the United States was also operated as a government-enforced cartel, in this instance by the Interstate Commerce

Commission (ICC).[17] The ICC established government-mandated routes and prices and imposed regulations that restricted trucking services (prohibiting trucks, for instance, from making a delivery and then picking up another delivery for the drive back).

After trucking was finally (partially) deregulated by the Motor Carrier Act of 1980, trucking prices fell by 25 percent in the first five years (and consumers benefited from lower prices for goods that were trucked); competition thrived; and more non-union truckers were hired. It wasn't just airlines and trucking where regulation benefited the regulated. Business historian Gabriel Kolko proved in his book, *The Triumph of Conservatism*, that the "progressive era" (1900-1916) regulatory forms, such as the creation of the Fed and the Federal Trade Commission, and the regulation of the meat industry, were in fact promoted by big business interests themselves.[18] Bankers wanted a national bank that could expand their lending abilities; large corporations favored the Food and Drug Act because of their (correct) belief that regulatory requirements would impose a disproportionate burden on their smaller competitors and deter others from entering the business in the first place; and antitrust laws have always been used to harass and punish companies that are too successful in meeting consumer demand.[19] Large corporations sought these regulatory institutions as a means of stifling competition, just as they did in the "public utilities" industries.

Socialists might claim to hate big business, but their regulatory state is one of the greatest defenders of big business ever created.

14

DESTROYING CAPITALISM BY SOCIALIZING CAPITAL

Marx and Engels wanted socialist governments to control financial capital. *The Communist Manifesto*'s fifth of ten planks calls for "Centralization of Credit in the banks of the state, by means of a national bank with state capital and an exclusive monopoly."[1] Capitalism cannot exist in any meaningful sense without private capital markets. One of the chief virtues of capitalism—indeed, perhaps *the* chief virtue—is that economic resources are constantly allocated and reallocated according to the wishes of consumers, which private lenders have to take into account. It was private capital markets, for instance, that funded the personal computer revolution, betting, correctly, that consumers would prefer computers to typewriters. Capitalists in a free market assess risk and demand a thousand times every day and are rewarded with profits or punished with losses depending on how well they serve consumers.

Socialists distrust all this spontaneous economic activity. They want a "planned" economy, designed by bureaucrats. And today, every government in the world has adopted the socialist platform to at least to some degree, most especially with national banks that centralize credit.

HOW SOCIALIST ARE U.S. CAPITAL MARKETS?

Ever since the creation of the Federal Reserve Board in 1913, the United States has met the first requirement of plank five of *The Communist Manifesto* calling for "a national bank." There were two other national banks in American history—the First (1791-1811) and Second (1816-1836) Banks of the United States, but the Second Bank was vetoed out of existence in the late 1830s by President Andrew Jackson, who charged the bank with corrupting politics; subsidizing a wealthy, politically connected class; and destabilizing the economy.[2]

The Fed has the ability to print money (or these days, create it electronically) to purchase government bonds. Not only does it put billions of dollars into circulation, but interest earned on the bonds goes to pay the salaries and perks of Federal Reserve employees, giving the Fed an obvious bias towards monetary inflation.

The Fed also indirectly subsidizes the private banking industry with its "reserve requirements" of how much currency a bank must hold in its vaults or with the Federal Reserve. These requirements are usually set between 2 percent and 10 percent. A 10 percent reserve requirement, for example, means that a bank can lend out $10 million by keeping $1 million in reserve.

Prior to the establishment of the Fed there were periods of competing currencies: some banks held higher levels of reserves (usually in gold or silver) than others, signifying to the public that the currency they issued was more stable and reliable. Banks with minimal reserves were suspect and were not very profitable or went bankrupt. Under the regime of competing currencies the more stable and responsible banks were rewarded with profits, while the less responsible ones incurred losses or bankruptcy. The Dix ("ten" in French) was a currency issued by a New Orleans bank in the nineteenth century that was so trusted that it was even used in Minnesota. This is where the word "Dixie" comes from—land of the Dix.

The Fed ended competing currencies by imposing a single reserve "requirement" on most banks (and was assisted by the National Currency Act of 1863 and 1864 that taxed currencies other than the greenback dollar). In essence, the Fed became the enforcer of a banking cartel, which, if it had been done by the banks themselves, would have violated federal antitrust laws prohibiting "conspiracies in restraint of trade" and the banks' managers could have been sent to prison.[3]

The Fed, like all central banks, is essentially a socialistic central-planning agency that claims to "stabilize" and "fine tune" the economy. No such central planning agency existed for much of American history. In the 124 years from the ratification of the U.S. Constitution in 1789 to the creation of the Fed in 1913, a national bank existed only for twenty years, or about 16 percent of the time. There was some regulation of branch banking, and the government periodically stopped banks from redeeming currency with gold or silver, but for the most part, the United States enjoyed a free market capital system, with no army of central planners.

Even though the Fed is charged with "stabilizing" the economy, it has in fact generated numerous boom-and-bust cycles. At the outset of the twenty-first century, the Fed flooded the markets with currency to drive interest rates toward zero. The Fed's easy-money policies were largely responsible for both the 2000 stock market bubble (and bust) and the housing bubble that exploded into the Great Recession of 2008. Even the Great Depression of the 1930s came on the heels of the Fed's expansionary monetary policies of the late 1920s that generated a stock market bubble followed by the famous crash of October 1929.[4]

The Fed's low-interest-rate policy is an attempt to impose price controls on interest, which in turn, inevitably encourages too much investment in houses, cars, the stock market, and many other industries *that is not justified by the market or consumer demand*. The Fed does this because it inflates economic growth, at least in the short term, but it does so at the cost of an incredible misallocation of resources or what Austrian School economists call "malinvestment." At some point reality sets in as supply far outstrips consumer demand, and the "bust" occurs, whether in housing or some other industry, throwing thousands, or tens of thousands, or hundreds of thousands, out of work and the economy into recession.

The Fed also contributes to what economists call "fiscal illusion"—making the cost of government seem much lower than it really is. If the public realized the true costs of government, it might oppose many more government programs than it does now. Every federal government program can be financed through either direct taxes, borrowing, or the Fed's creation of money. Tax finance is the most visible, for obvious reasons. Government borrowing defers the presumed cost of current government spending programs to the future, while simply printing more money through the central bank, creating the impression that government programs are free. As Adam Smith said, with tax finance there would be fewer wars, and wars that were fought would be shorter-lived. The same can be said of all other government programs financed by money created by the Fed.

There is also a large literature in economics on what are called "political business cycles."[5] By at least partially financing government programs through printing money, the Fed assists incumbent politicians by pumping up government spending just before elections. Every congressional district is showered with federal grants to build new schools, repair roads, hire more police and firefighters, and so on. This generates even *more instability* in the economy, contrary to the hollow claims by central bank apologists that it "stabilizes" the economy. There is a false sense of growth and prosperity before the elections, and then often an economic retrenchment afterwards. Then the cycle repeats itself in the next election year.

Monetary economists George Selgin, William Lastrapes, and Lawrence H. White assessed the Fed's performance over its first one hundred years and concluded the following: the Fed's history is characterized by *more* rather than fewer episodes of economic instability than in the decades leading up to the creation of the Fed; the Fed's performance is inferior to the banking system that preceded it, known as the National Banking System; *the U.S. dollar lost 95 percent of its purchasing power since the creation of the Fed,* compared to a stable purchasing power of the dollar from the late eighteenth century to 1913; the Fed has eliminated deflation, which was a happy occurrence in the eyes of consumers for the entire period from the end of the American Civil War to the turn of the twentieth century; and recessions have been more severe and longer-lasting since the creation of the Fed.[6]

In addition to all of these failures, after the "Great Recession" of 2008, the Fed financed massive bailouts of financial firms that had made billions of dollars of bad business decisions. Capitalism is a profit-and-loss system, not an "I-keep-all-the-profits-but-the-public-covers-all-my-losses" system. Socialized losses and privatized profits is a corruption of markets and was a hallmark of twentieth-century economic fascism, an economic model to which western socialists seem eager to return.[7]

The Fed regulates virtually every aspect of America's financial markets. For example, in one of the Fed's publications entitled "The Federal Reserve System: Purposes and Functions," the central bank boasts of its responsibilities to regulate bank-holding companies, state-chartered banks, foreign branches of member banks, edge and agreement corporations, U.S. state-licensed branches, agencies, and representative offices of foreign banks, nonbanking activities of foreign banks, national banks, savings banks, nonbank subsidiaries of bank holding companies, thrift holding companies, financial reporting procedures, accounting policies of banks, business "continuity" in case of economic emergencies, consumer protection laws, securities dealings of banks, information technology used by banks, foreign investment by banks, foreign lending by banks, branch banking, bank mergers and acquisitions, who may own a bank, capital "adequacy standards," extensions of credit for the purchase of securities, equal opportunity lending, mortgage disclosure information, reserve requirements, electronic funds transfers, inter-bank liabilities, Community Reinvestment Act sub-prime lending demands, all international banking operations, consumer leasing, privacy of consumer financial information, payments on demand deposits, "fair credit" reporting, transactions between member banks and their affiliates, truth in lending, and truth in savings.[8]

Financial markets in the United States are also regulated by the Federal Trade Commission, Consumer Product Safety Commission, Commodity Futures Trading Commission, Farm Credit Administration, Federal Deposit Insurance Corporation, U.S. Consumer Financial Protection Bureau, Securities and Exchange Commission, Securities Investor Protection Corporation, Small Business Administration, National Credit Union Administration, Comptroller of the Currency, Financial Stability Oversight Council, Office of Financial Research, and the Financial Industries Regulatory Authority.[9]

If that weren't enough, there are dozens of state and local government regulatory agencies that also regulate financial market transactions.

In addition, the 2010 "Dodd-Frank Wall Street Reform and Consumer Protection Act" mandated (for starters) 243 new regulatory rules affecting financial markets in the U.S.[10]

The United States has no shortage of financial regulations. What it has is a shortage of truly free markets in finance and banking.

DISTORTING MARKETS
WITH SOCIALIZED LENDING

Beginning with the now-defunct Reconstruction Finance Corporation, created by the Herbert Hoover administration in 1932, the federal government has been heavily involved in directly extending loans and loan guarantees to myriad businesses and individuals, including banks, to the tune of hundreds of billions of dollars each year. (A loan guarantee is when the government promises to pay off the loan if the borrower defaults, thereby reducing the interest rate on the loan by eliminating the risk to the lender.) By definition, whenever government extends a loan or loan guarantee to a business, it is expanding the activity of that business beyond what private capital markets would do. The subsidy involved is the difference between the free-market rate of interest that the borrower would pay and the government-guaranteed rate, which is always lower. In such instances the government is effectively vetoing the opinions of consumers, who are not purchasing the product or service in great enough numbers (if at all) to justify *any* loan. Politics inevitably replaces economics and plays the predominant role in determining who gets the government-subsidized loans, which are essentially used as vote-buying and campaign-contribution-soliciting tools by members of Congress and by presidents.

The amount of loans and loan guarantees handed out by government, substituting political preferences and whims for economic viability as the main lending criterion, is staggering. For example, in less than two years the Obama administration guaranteed $100 billion in loans to its pet "green energy" businesses. One of them, Solyndra, a solar panel manufacturing company, went bankrupt in 2011 after receiving a highly publicized $536 million loan guarantee by the Obama administration in 2009.[11] Democratic fund-raisers, given jobs in the Obama administration, routinely steered "green" loan guarantees to businesses they had been associated with prior to joining the administration.[12] Unlike in a free-market, *their* private capital wasn't put at risk, the taxpayers' money was.

A hallmark of socialist countries is that one must be politically "connected" to have any hope of succeeding in "business." Capital markets are organized according to political, as opposed to economic, criteria. It should be no surprise then that socialist economies, for all their "rational" planning, are inevitably irrational and bankrupt. The more America socializes its capital markets through Federal Reserve central planning, regulation, and politically favored loans and loan guarantees, the more it will destroy its heritage of prosperity.

15

IS SOCIALISM REALLY THE BEST WAY TO ORGANIZE SCHOOLS?

I magine that the grocery industry was organized in the following way: every residence is assigned by the government to the nearest neighborhood grocery store where it must purchase its groceries. There are heavy penalties for anyone caught shopping at an alternative grocery store. All groceries are paid for with an annual lump-sum tax collected by the local government. Anyone can then walk into her assigned grocery store and pick up whatever she wants, and local governments boast about their "free public groceries."

It is possible to shop elsewhere, but one must then pay twice—once with the grocery tax, and then a second time by paying cash for the alternative groceries. Consequently, only the more affluent can afford to have any real freedom of choice.

All employees of the grocery stores are paid the same according to whichever seniority group they belong to. More seniority means higher pay, but everyone with the same seniority level is paid the same. If there are too many checkout clerks and not enough butchers, the public employees' grocers union prohibits paying butchers more to alleviate the butcher shortage; it also opposes merit pay. That would be un-egalitarian.

It is almost impossible to fire a grocery store employee for any reason except criminality. Depending on the city, most grocery employees received job tenure after three years.

Grocery store employees who are grossly incompetent and negligent are routinely promoted up and out, since they can't be fired, and given jobs at the central grocery administrative offices: hence the saying, "those who can stack shelves, do; those who can't become central grocery administrators." Because they are "public servants" they are granted lavish taxpayer-funded pensions—far more lavish than anything most private sector taxpayers have—and liberal vacation time, and the salaries for administrators are far higher than they would merit in a private business.

If the grocery stores are so badly run that food rots on the shelves and their spending exceeds their budgets, or if the grocery workers go on strike, the grocery tax is simply increased, because every politician wants to be in favor of "free groceries;" no one wants to be an "enemy of the poor and the hungry," and certainly no one wants the grocery stores to close down, even temporarily, because of the stores' virtual monopoly.

I once presented this scenario to a class of undergraduate economics students and asked them whether a grocery system like this would be very efficient at holding down food costs and providing good food products. Of course they laughed. And when I asked if the system sounded familiar, a twenty-year-old college junior blurted out "Communism!" After a few moments of silence another student said "public schools!" They were both right.

Government-run public schools suffer the same problems as any other socialist enterprise. A private school has to compete for students. If a private school fails to serve the needs and expectations of its customers (parents), it loses money, it loses market share, and it could eventually go out of business. A government-run school enjoys a virtual monopoly, especially among the poor, who can't afford a private school;

and as with all monopolies, the convenience of administrators and employees comes before the needs of the customers, because the customers will always be there. They have no choice.

As with all government enterprises, the incentives are perverse: the worse the job they do in teaching children, the *more* money that is typically given to the public schools, because everyone wants to "improve" education, even if there is rarely, if ever, any evidence that the additional money is helping students to learn more rather than simply paying failing teachers and administrators more and providing the schools with more facilities or programs of dubious educational value. Imagine if corporations behaved in this way— *raising* prices—in response to consumers walking away in droves because of their tasteless food, dangerous automobiles, shoddy clothing, or whatever. It sounds absurd, yet that is the *modus operandi* of *all* public schools everywhere.

Affluent areas have better public schools than poor areas not because the former have more tax money than the latter, but because affluent parents can afford to send their children to private schools. That mere threat of competition forces public schools in affluent areas to do better, despite the education bureaucracy. As with so many socialistic schemes, the public school near-monopoly on education hurts the poor most of all.

More money for poor schools is not the answer. Per-student spending in U.S public schools was more than two-and-a-half times higher in 2013 than it was in 1970, in inflation-adjusted dollars ($4,060 compared to $10,700).[1] Real, inflation-adjusted spending increased substantially in every state and the District of Columbia (which spent $17,953 per student in 2013).[2] During that time, national reading scores remained flat and the graduation rate increased by only a miniscule percentage.[3] The black student graduation rate lags behind the white public school student graduation rate by about twenty percentage points (59.1 percent to 80.6 percent in one recent year),[4] which is not surprising when you consider that black students are far less likely to attend public schools that have to compete with nearby private schools. A Cato Institute study found that after a near tripling of per-student spending on public schools in real, inflation-adjusted dollars, and a more than doubling of public school employees over forty years, student achievement in both math and verbal skills actually *declined*.[5]

One would be hard pressed to find *any* private enterprise that had declining production, performance, or sales after massive infusions of capital (outside of government-subsidized businesses like Solyndra). Would anyone expect a restaurant that doubled its staff to serve *fewer* dinners? Would a grocery store chain that built more stores sell *fewer* groceries? Would UPS deliver *fewer* packages if it hired a thousand more drivers? Only in monopolistic, socialistic enterprises like the public schools does one find the absurdity of paying far more for the service and getting nothing in return.

No more than half of all the increased taxpayer funding for public schools ends up in the classroom (teachers' salaries, instructional materials, and so on).[6] The rest is eaten up by layers and layers of bureaucracy, not to mention all the capital spending on buildings and facilities. Private schools have to spend their money efficiently, because they operate for profit. Public schools actually have incentives to spend more—to show off their shiny new buildings or to set spending ever higher to justify even more budget increases—but no incentive to spend efficiently; efficient spending, after all, would mean fewer bureaucrats, fewer bureaucratic regulations, and pay based on performance.

Government-run schools are increasingly weighed down by bureaucratic mandates imposed by government at all levels, including the federal government, which is becoming an ever larger source of taxpayer funding of government schools. In many states there is so much detailed regulation of the local schools that teachers are given orders regarding how many minutes per day they must teach history, math, and other subjects.

The government-run schools in the socialist regimes of the twentieth century were indoctrination academies that taught obedience to the state. Plank ten of the ten-point agenda in *The Communist Manifesto* called for "Free education for all children in public schools."[7] The twenty-five-point program of the Nazi Party similarly demanded that "The conception of the State Idea...must be taught in the schools from the very beginning."[8] Government-run schools in democratic countries, being in the hands of politicians and government bureaucrats, inevitably become propaganda factories. Murray Rothbard showed in his book *Education, Free and Compulsory*, that the founding fathers of the public school movement in America were themselves ideological egalitarians and statists.[9] Mandates like Common Core, supported by the federal Department of Education, or state mandates like California's Fair Education Act (popularly known as the "gay history bill"), are imposed in the name of "standards" or "fairness," but in fact they are often shackles on how and what teachers can teach and students can think. They can do this because schooling is *compulsory*, because many parents consider that they don't have a choice of schools, and every mandate strips parents of *control* of their schools, putting more power in the hands of bureaucrats. Among the virtues of a free market in education would be not just competition on price and performance, but competition for best suiting the needs and interests of parents and students; as the customers, *they* would be in charge. Schools would be in the business of best serving parents and their children or going bust.

Private schools, or homeschoolers, are not beyond the reach of state of course, as they have to meet "certification" requirements or testing requirements and so forth, but at least they stand as reminders to the state that children belong to their parents, not the government.

Public schools, on the other hand, because they are run by the government, are incubators of political correctness and inculcate statist assumptions, including the idea that it is normal for the state to have a near-monopoly on education. Rothbard went so far as to say that government-run education produces "a race of passive sheep-like followers of the state" and teaches "the doctrine of state supremacy."[10]

The never-ending quest for uniformity, common cores, and "equality" destroys independent thought, almost by definition. As H. L. Mencken once wrote: "The most dangerous man to any government is the man who is able to think things out for himself, without regard to the prevailing superstitions and taboos. Almost inevitably he comes to the conclusion that the government he lives under is dishonest, insane, and intolerable."[11]

16

SOCIALIST MYTHS AND SUPERSTITIONS ABOUT CAPITALISM

I t is easy to attack an institution if you define it in the most preposterous way possible. For well over one hundred years, socialists have built endless capitalist straw men to attack and have attacked them so often that they hope by sheer repetition people will actually believe their socialist arguments. A prime example is the socialist mantra of "People not Profit" or "Production for Use, Not for Profit."[1] Capitalists, allegedly, are only interested in profit and ignore the needs of "people." This is the exact opposite of the truth.

No one can succeed in a system of free-market capitalism without serving "the people." Competition in a market economy is all about better meeting the needs of customers. Businesses that excel at meeting customer demand are rewarded with profits, those that don't suffer losses.

It is *government* that is guilty of ignoring the needs of the people, not capitalism. Governments simply announce to the public, "Here, we believe that you need this, and we will force you to pay for it." "The fundamental principle of capitalism," wrote Ludwig von Mises, is that competitive businesses produce "almost exclusively to satisfy the wants of the masses. Enterprises producing luxury goods solely for the well-to-do can never attain the magnitude of big businesses."[2] The so-called "power" of big businesses in the free market comes entirely from "the people" who voluntarily purchase their products by "voting" with their dollars. And that "power" can be extinguished on a moment's notice, as soon as a competing entrepreneur comes along with a cheaper or better-quality product. Consumer sovereignty reigns in a market economy.

The "power" of big government (or any government), in stark contrast, comes entirely from the government's ability to coerce and force the people to bend to its will with intimidation, threats, and violence. That is always the *modus operandi* of socialism. When the Socialist Party USA or Democratic Socialists of America urge the greater politicization of all aspects of society, as they do on their websites with endless happy talk about "democracy," this is really what they mean: subjecting more and more of society to bureaucratic plans and mandates imposed by a small political elite and enforced by threats, intimidation, and violence—the common everyday tools of all socialist governments. When the Democratic Socialists of America say, "Democracy and socialism go hand in hand," what they mean is that they want every aspect of life to be politicized and brought into the realm of government supervision and control.

Capitalist entrepreneurs gain wealth by providing products and services that people buy of their own free will. John D. Rockefeller started out penniless and became the wealthiest man of his time by producing refined petroleum products at ever cheaper prices. In the process, he created tens of thousands of jobs, and billions of dollars of wealth (in both income and products) for the American economy. Rockefeller invested his profits in myriad businesses and industries, creating even more jobs and prosperity, and was a major philanthropist. (It was Rockefeller's wealth that founded the University of Chicago, among other things.) Entrepreneurs who became wealthy through free-market competition *always* benefit their society through creating wealth and jobs, and almost invariably are leaders in charitable giving.[3] As Ludwig von Mises wrote:

The history of capitalism as it has operated in the last two hundred years in the realm of Western civilization is the record of a steady rise in the wage earners' standard of living. The inherent mark of capitalism is that it is mass production for mass consumption directed by the most energetic and far-sighted individuals, unflaggingly aiming at improvement. Its driving force is the profit motive, the instrumentality of which forces the businessman constantly to provide the consumers with more, better, and cheaper amenities. An excess of profits over losses can appear only in a progressing economy and only to the extent to which the masses' standard of living improves. Thus capitalism is the system under which the keenest and most agile minds are driven to promote to the best of their abilities the welfare of the laggard many.[4]

THE MYTH OF "SUBSISTENCE WAGES"

One of the oldest socialist myths, invented by Karl Marx himself, is that capitalism's "labor exploitation" dooms "the working class" to subsistence-level wages.

This, too, is the exact opposite of the truth: capitalism has been the main cause of *increases* in wages, improved working conditions, and prosperity for the working class—and all other "classes." It was under *socialism* in the twentieth century that the working class was paid near starvation-level wages and *forced* to toil in horrendous conditions. The last thing in the world the "working class" needs is socialism and economic stagnation.

During what historians call America's "first industrial revolution" (1820–1860) the average worker's paycheck increased by 60 to 90 percent.[5] During the "second industrial revolution" (1860–1890) real wages (adjusted for inflation) rose another 50 percent while the average work week was shortened.[6] While wages went *up*, production of new and better products improved dramatically, and prices went *down* with price *deflation* from the end of the Civil War to the turn of the century.

The shorter work week, which averaged sixty-one hours in 1870, was much more the result of capitalist investment and technology that improved productivity than it was the result of laws and regulations. These only confirmed the progress being made by capitalism. As Ludwig von Mises noted, "The 19th century's labor legislation by and large achieved nothing more than to provide a legal ratification for changes that the interplay of market forces had brought about previously."[7] Capitalism, as economists Michael Cox and Richard

Alm explain, is the reason, "American workers have become more efficient, applying technology, better tools, and improved skills to produce more goods and services on the job."[8] As workers become more productive, employers, in turn, compete for their services by offering them better pay and/or shorter hours.

Socialists like to argue that under capitalism the rich get richer and the poor get poorer; these days, it's usually a matter of presenting statistics on "income distribution" to show that the top earners' "share of national income" has gone up, while the bottom 10 or 20 percent of income earners have seen their share stay the same or go down. To get to this conclusion you have to assume that *the same people* are somehow stuck in an economic rut at the bottom of the income scale. Economists Michael Cox and Richard Alm exposed this by citing a University of Michigan study that tracked more than 50,000 Americans for three decades to discern the extent of economic mobility in America. They found that very few people are "stuck" at the bottom of the economic ladder; most rise quickly. Among their findings:

- More than three-fourths of families in the bottom fifth of income distribution in 1975 had made their way up to the *two highest* income quintiles in 1991.

- The poorest families made the largest gains. Those who started in the bottom 20 percent in 1975 had an inflation-adjusted gain in annual income of $27,745 by 1991; those who started in the top 20 percent in 1975 also improved, but only by $4,354.

- Less than 1 percent of the sample population remained in the bottom 20 percent during the 1975-1991 period.

- More than half of the families who were in the bottom 20 percent in 1975 made it to a higher bracket within four years.[9]

The greatest engine for economic mobility, progress, and opportunity is capitalism; and there is no way that socialists can get around their own history of economic stagnation and failure.

THE MYTH OF THE ABUSIVE FACTORY

Working conditions in nineteenth-century factories were often horrendous by modern-day standards, and socialists have used this fact to make the case that the invention of the factory system was harmful to workers, both physically and economically. But comparing working conditions in nineteenth-century factories to today's working conditions is not the proper comparison. The proper comparison is with *what the workers left behind* when they left the farms to work in the factories. Because they *voluntarily* left the farms for the factories, it is obvious that *they* believed that their wages and working conditions were improved by doing so. Factory work, as difficult as it was, was obviously an improvement over back-breaking, sixteen-hour days of farm labor for miniscule wages. Interestingly, it was not socialist propagandists who first put forth the arguments about how factory work supposedly reduced the economic well-being of workers, but the landed aristocracy that was incensed by the higher wages paid by industry. Because the factories were offering higher wages than what could be earned as a farm laborer, the landed aristocracy was forced to compete by offering higher wages to farm workers.[10]

In the early days of capitalism it was not uncommon for mothers to bring some of their older children with them to work in the factories. This sounds deplorable by today's standards, but, again, the alternative was farm labor at lower, and often more uncertain, wages;

and child labor laws were, again, a result of capitalist economic progress, of increasing wages and wealth so that it was no longer necessary for families to put their children to work.

THE MYTH OF THE "ROBBER BARONS"

For more than a century, socialists have smeared successful nineteenth-century American entrepreneurs as "robber barons." These men were anything but "robbers" or "barons."

Cornelius Vanderbilt got his start in business by breaking up a steamboat monopoly on the Hudson River enjoyed by crony capitalist Robert Fulton, who had secured a thirty-year monopoly license from the state of New York.[11] Vanderbilt was hired by New York businessman Thomas Gibbons to defy the state's steamboat monopoly, and he succeeded. He cut the fare from New York to Hartford eventually to zero and made money by selling food and drinks on the ships. The U.S. Supreme Court ended the steamboat monopoly licensing scheme with its 1824 ruling in *Gibbons vs. Ogden*, maintaining that only the federal government, not state governments, can regulate inter-state trade under the Commerce Clause of the U.S. Constitution. This was a classic case of a genuine free-market entrepreneur (Vanderbilt) out-competing a crony capitalist favored by government (Fulton). Vanderbilt of course went on to become extremely successful in the railroad industry.

James J. Hill built a transcontinental railroad, The Great Northern, without any government subsidies and out-competed all the government-subsidized crony capitalists who operated the Union Pacific and Central Pacific Railroads.[12] While the latter corporations were given hundreds of miles of land and per-mile building subsidies by the U.S. government, Hill boasted of having built The Great Northern "without any government aid, even the right of way, through hundreds of miles of public lands, being paid for in cash."[13] The Great Northern became the "most profitable of all the world's major railroads." Hill refused to join in price-fixing cartels and instead steadily reduced the rates he charged. He generated good will with local communities along his route in myriad ways, such as donating land for parks, schools, and churches and helping to educate farmers in the latest developments in agricultural science.[14]

The crony capitalist railroads, on the other hand, were built in extraordinarily wasteful ways since all of their waste and cost over-runs were subsidized by the government. Indeed, much of the wastefulness was *required* by the government, subsidizing unprofitable small rail lines in certain congressional districts, in order to secure votes in Congress for more subsidies. The Union Pacific and Central Pacific were eventually exposed as the instigators of one of the then biggest political corruption scandals in American history, the Crédit Mobilier scandal.

Like James J. Hill and many other successful free-market capitalists of the nineteenth century, John D. Rockefeller started from nothing. His Standard Oil Company was praised by even his harshest and most envious critics as "a marvelous example of economy" in business.[15] Because of Standard Oil's outstanding efficiency and competitiveness, its share of the refined petroleum market increased from 4 percent in 1870 to 25 percent in 1874 and 85 percent by 1880. It did this by cutting the cost of refining a gallon of oil from three cents to less than half a cent, and passing the cost reductions on to its customers. The price of refined oil plummeted from thirty cents a gallon in 1869 to eight cents by 1885.[16]

Rockefeller was extremely generous with his employees, paying them more than the competition and rewarding his managers with bonuses and time off for good performance. Consequently, his workers were more productive and he was rarely slowed down by strikes.

THE MYTH OF "PREDATORY PRICING"

Socialists often charge that capitalists use "predatory pricing" to drive out competition and thus create monopolies that can then exploit consumers with high prices. One problem with this theory, however, is that no one has ever found a monopoly that was created in this way.[17] Socialist folklore has it that John D. Rockefeller was a "monopolist," but when his company was broken up by the antitrust authorities, he had more than 300 competitors, which is hardly anyone's definition of a monopoly.

The reason why no one has ever found a monopoly created through predatory pricing is because no business leader would intentionally lose money *for years* in the uncertain hope that he might bankrupt his competitors and with the dangerous possibility that even if he somehow succeeded in establishing a monopoly, it wouldn't be permanent, as new competitors tried to undercut his monopoly pricing. There are many other less risky ways to make money, such as simply expanding one's core business. As for the hoary accusations that Standard Oil practiced predatory pricing, economist John McGee studied the entire Standard Oil antitrust case and concluded in the *Journal of Law and Economics* that there was no evidence in the trial that Standard Oil ever attempted predatory pricing; it was merely very good at old-fashioned price-cutting competition.[18]

THE CAPITALISM-CAUSES-WAR MYTH

Socialists like to allege that capitalism causes war. Capitalist economies, they say, produce too much for domestic consumption, and therefore invade other countries to dump products on their markets. One early twentieth-century proponent of this idea was the Marxist John A. Hobson, author of the book *Imperialism*. Lenin himself praised Hobson and repeated the notion in his *Imperialism: The Highest Stage of Capitalism*.

Like so many other socialist myths about capitalism, the truth is exactly the opposite. War and capitalism are in reality opposite extremes. Free market capitalism is all about trade, including international trade; it is about the free exchange of goods and ideas, which encourages peace and mutual understanding. There is an old saying, sometimes credited to the nineteenth-century French economist Frédéric Bastiat, that "If goods don't cross borders, armies will." Free trade encourages peaceful cooperation, while restraints on capitalism, like protectionism and tariffs, can create "trade wars" that become real wars.

The height of protectionism, or economic nationalism, is "autarky," a policy of attempting to be economically self-sufficient as a nation, producing everything a population needs from domestic sources. Nazi Germany was one country that followed this policy, and since Germany did not have enough resources to achieve economic self- sufficiency, it invaded other countries to expropriate the resources it needed.[19] Germany's national socialists were not alone of course; governments have waged wars of economic conquest for centuries, but capitalism— which encourages international *free* trade—is almost by definition not the reason; wars of economic conquest are almost invariably the result of some variant of mercantilism, socialism, or autarky, three economic theories that put the interests of the state, which controls the military, first.

It is essential for citizens of a free and prosperous society to understand enough about economic logic (and economic reality) to see through socialist myths. I hope this book has gone some way towards helping expose just a few of the myriad problems of socialism and restoring the ideal of free markets and human freedom.

NOTES

1

1. YouGov America, "Democrats More Divided on Socialism," https://today.yougov.com/news/2016/01/28/democrats-remain-divided-socialism/.
2. Marion Smith, "How Did America Forget What 'Socialist' Means?" *Politico*, March 22, 2016.
3. Ibid.
4. See www.TaxFoundation.org.
5. Friedrich Hayek, *The Road to Serfdom* (Chicago: University of Chicago Press, 1976).
6. Ludwig von Mises, *Socialism: An Economic and Sociological Analysis* (Auburn: Ludwig von Mises Institute, 2015).

7.   Mamta Badkar,"Ten Hyper-Inflation Stories of the 20th Century," *Business Insider*, March 19, 2011, http://businessinsider.com/10-hyperinflation-stories-of-the-20th-century-2011-3?op=1.

8.   Madsen Pirie, "Ten Myths about Margaret Thatcher," Adam Smith Institute, April 15, 2013, http://www.adamsmith.org/blog/politics-government/ten-myths-about-margaret-thatcher/.

9.   Badkar,"Ten Hyper-Inflation Stories of the 20th Century."

10.   Charles Scaliger, "Can Some Socialism Be a Good Thing?," *The New American*, January 28, 2016, 15.

11.   Ashok Rudra, *Prasanta Chandra Mahalanobis: A Biography* (Oxford: Oxford University Press, 1996).

12.   George Ayittey, *Africa Betrayed* (New York: Palgrave MacMillan, 1994).

13.   George Ayittey, "Betrayal: Why Socialism Failed in Africa," Foundation for Economic Education, December 24, 2008, http://fee.org/resources/betrayal-why-socialism-failed-in-africa/.

14.   Ibid., 2.

15.   Ibid.

16.   Ibid., 4.

17.   Scalinger, "Can Some Socialism Be a Good Thing?"

2

1.   George Ayittey, *Africa in Chaos* (New York: Palgrave MacMillan, 1999).

2.   "George Percy's Account of the Voyage to Virginia and the Colony's First Days," in *The Old Dominion*

in the Seventeenth Century: A Documentary History of Virginia, 1606-1689, Warren M. Billings, ed. (Chapel Hill: University of North Carolina Press, 1975), 22–26.

3. Ibid., 28.
4. Ibid.
5. Philip A. Bruce, *Economic History of Virginia in the Seventeenth Century* (New York: Macmillan, 1907), 212.
6. Matthew Page Andrews, *Virginia, The Old Dominion*, vol. 1 (Richmond: Dietz Press, 1949), 59.
7. William Bradford, *Of Plymouth Plantation, 1620–1647* (New York: Knopf, 2002), 116.
8. Ibid., 120.
9. Jeremy Atak and Peter Passell, *A New Economic View of American History* (New York: Norton, 1994), 50.
10. Murray N. Rothbard, "The End of Socialism and the Calculation Debate Revisited," Mises Daily, December 8, 2006, https://mises.org/library/end-socialism-and-calculation-debate-revisited.
11. David Osterfeld, "Socialism and Incentives," Foundation for Economic Education, November 1, 1986, http://fee.org/articles/socialism-and-incentives/.
12. Ibid., 5.
13. Jean-Louis Panné et al., *The Black Book of Communism: Crimes, Terror, Repression* (Cambridge: Harvard University Press, 1999).
14. Friedrich Hayek, "The Use of Knowledge in Society," *American Economic Review*, 35 no. 4 (September 1945): 519–530.

15. Ludwig von Mises, *Socialism: An Economic and Sociological Analysis* (Auburn: Ludwig von Mises Institute, 2015).

16. Ludwig von Mises, *Human Action: The Scholars' Edition* (Auburn: Ludwig von Mises Institute, 2010).

17. Robert Heilbroner, "The Triumph of Capitalism," *The New Yorker*, January 16, 1989.

∃

1. R. J. Rummel, *Death by Government* (New Brunswick: Transaction Publishers, 1997).

2. Daniel Lapin, *Thou Shall Prosper: The Ten Commandments for Making Money* (New York: Wiley, 2002).

3. Ludwig von Mises, *Human Action: The Scholars' Edition* (Auburn: Ludwig von Mises Institute, 1998), 157.

4. H.L. Mencken, *A Mencken Crestomathy* (New York: Alfred A. Knopf, 1949), 145.

5. Karl Marx, quoted in Alexander Gray, *The Socialist Tradition* (London: Longmans, Green, 1947), 328.

6. Leon Trotsky, quoted in Ludwig von Mises, *Socialism: An Economic and Sociological Analysis* (Auburn: Ludwig von Mises Institute, 2010), 164.

7. Ludwig von Mises, *The Anticapitalistic Mentality* (New York: Van Nostrand, 1956).

8. Ibid., 25.

9. Ibid., 40.

10. L.P. Hartley, *Facial Justice* (Oxford: Oxford Paperbacks, 1987).

11. Kurt Vonnegut Jr., "Harrison Bergeron," in *Welcome to the Monkey House* (New York: Dell, 1970), 7.
12. Ibid., 6.
13. Murray N. Rothbard, "Egalitarianism as a Revolt Against Nature," LewRockwell.com, http://www.lewrockwell.com/1970/01/murray-n-rothbard/were-not-equal/.

4

1. See "Privatization," Reason Foundation, www.reason.org/areas/topic/privatization.
2. Thomas Borcherding, *Budgets and Bureaucrats: The Sources of Government Growth* (Durham: Duke University Press, 1977).
3. Susan Jones, "WH: Food Stamps 'Are Boosting the Economy,'" cnsnews.com, December 2, 2013, http://www.cnsnews.com/news/article/susan-jones/wh-food-stamps-are-boosting-economy.
4. Murray N. Rothbard, *Power and Market: Government and the Economy* (New York: Sheed Andrews and McMeel, 1977), 214.
5. Chris Megerian, Matt Stevens, and Bettina Boxall, "Brown Orders California's First Mandatory Water Restrictions,"*Los Angeles Times*, April 1, 2015.
6. Victor Davis Hanson, "Why California's Drought Was Completely Preventable," *National Review*, April 30, 2015, http://www.nationalreview.com/article/417685/why-californias-drought-was-completely-preventable-victor-davis-hanson.

7. Rothbard, *Power and Market*, 215.
8. Ibid., 219-220.
9. Adam Summers, "Comparing Private Sector and Government Worker Salaries," Reason Foundation, May 10, 2010, http://reason.org/news/show/public-sector-private-sector-salary.
10. Ibid.
11. See Ludwig von Mises, *Bureaucracy* (Westport: Arlington House, 1969); Anthony Downs, *Inside Bureaucracy* (New York: Scott Foresman, 1967); William Niskanen, *Bureaucracy and Representative Government* (Piskataway: Aldine Transaction, 2007); and Randy T. Simmons, *Beyond Politics: The Roots of Government Failure* (Oakland: Independent Institute, 2011).

5

1. Hayek, *The Road to Serfdom*, 158.
2. Ibid.
3. *Examining the History and Legality of Executive Branch Czars, Before the United States Senate Committee on the Judiciary*, 111th Cong. (2009) (Testimony of Mathew Spalding, Vice President, American Studies and Director, B. Kenneth Simon Center for Principles and Politics, The Heritage Foundation), http://www.heritage.org/research/testimony/examining-the-history-and-legality-of-executive-branch-czars.
4. Hayek, *The Road to Serfdom*, 159.
5. Ibid.
6. Ibid.

7.   Ibid., 160.
8.   Ibid., 161.
9.   Ibid.
10.   Ibid., 166.
11.   Ibid., 168.
12.   Ibid., 173.
13.   Ibid., 176.
14.   Panné et al.,*The Black Book of Communism: Crimes, Terror, Repression.*
15.   Ibid., 4.
16.   Ibid., 5.
17.   Rummel, *Death by Government*, 112–113.
18.   Ibid., 86.
19.   Ibid., 80.
20.   Ibid., 81.
21.   Panné et al.,*The Black Book of Communism*, 378.

6

1.   Bruce Caldwell, ed., *The Road to Serfdom: Text and Documents: The Definitive Edition* (Chicago: University of Chicago Press, 2007).
2.   Ibid., 245.
3.   Ibid., 246.
4.   Ibid.
5.   Ibid.
6.   Ibid.
7.   Ibid., 80.
8.   Ludwig von Mises, *Liberalism,* http://mises.org/library/liberalism-classical-tradition/html.
9.   Benito Mussolini, *Fascism: Doctrine and Institutions* (New York: Howard Fertig, Inc., 1968).

10. Ibid., 22.
11. Ibid., 29.
12. Ibid., 21.
13. Fausto Pitigliani, *The Italian Corporative State* (New York: MacMillan, 1934), x.
14. Ibid., 96.
15. Mussolini, *Fascism*, 70.
16. Gaetano Salvemini, *Under the Axe of Fascism* (New York: Viking Press, 1936), 380.
17. Paul Lensch, "Three Years of World Revolution," quoted in Hayek, *The Road to Serfdom* (Chicago: University of Chicago Press, 1976), 176.
18. Adolf Hitler, *Mein Kampf* (Boston: Houghton Mifflin, 1943), 297.
19. Erik von Kuehnelt-Leddihn, *Leftism Revisited* (Washington, DC: Regnery Gateway, 1990).

7

1. Stephan Karlsson, "The Sweden Myth," Mises Daily, August 7, 2006, https://mises.org/library/sweden-myth.
2. Julian Simon, *The Ultimate Resource* (Princeton: Princeton University Press, 1983).
3. Karlsson, "The Swedish Myth," 2.
4. Ibid., 3.
5. Ibid.
6. Per Bylund, "Stagnating Swedish Socialism," Mises Daily, January 11, 2011, https://mises.org/library/stagnating-socialist-sweden, 1.
7. Karlsson, "The Sweden Myth," 6.
8. Bylund, "Stagnating Socialist Sweden,"1.

9. Ibid., 2.
10. Karlsson, "The Sweden Myth, 8.
11. Per Bylund, "How the Welfare State Corrupted Sweden," Mises Daily, May 31, 2006, https://mises.org/library/how-welfare-state-corrupted-sweden.
12. Ibid., 7.
13. Ibid.
14. Ibid., 9.
15. Yonathan Amselem "How Modern Sweden Profits from the Success of Its Free-Market History," Mises Daily, October 16, 2015, https://mises.org/library/how-modern-sweden-profits-success-its-free-market-history.
16. Ibid., 3.
17. Per Henrik Hansen, "Denmark: Potemkin Village," Mises Daily, February 28, 2002, https://mises.org/library/denmark-potemkin-village.
18. Ibid., 4.
19. Ibid., 5.

8

1. Ludwig von Mises, *Socialism: An Economic and Sociological Analysis* (Auburn: Ludwig von Mises Institute, 2015).
2. Marvin Olasky, *The Tragedy of American Compassion* (Washington, DC: Regnery Gateway, 1994).
3. Charles Murray, *In Pursuit: Of Happiness and Good Government* (New York: Simon & Schuster, 1988), 275.
4. Ibid., 278.

5.   Charles Murray, *Losing Ground: American Social Policy, 1950-1980* (New York: Basic Books) 1084.

6.   Ibid., 65.

7.   Benda Cronin, "Worker or Welfare: What Pays More?," *Wall Street Journal*, August 19, 2013, http://blogs.wsj.com/economics/2013/09/19/work-or-welfare-what-pays-more/.

8.   Michael Tanner, "Ending Welfare," *Wall Street Journal* http://blogs.wsj.com/economics/2013/09/19/work-or-welfare-what-pays-more/; Michael Tanner, *Ending Welfare as We Know It,* Cato Institute, July 7, 1994, http://object.cato.org/sites/cato.org/files/pubs/pdf/pa212.pdf.

9.   Murray, *Losing Ground,* 185.

10.   Richard Vedder and Lowell Galloway, *The War on the Poor* (Lewiston: Institute for Policy Innovation, 1992).

11.   Tanner, *Ending Welfare as We Know It.*

12.   Murray, *Losing Ground,* 129.

13.   Gretchen Livingston, "Fewer than Half of U.S. Kids Today Live in a 'Traditional' Family," Pew Research Center FactTank, December 22, 2014, http://www.pewresearch.org/fact-tank/2014/12/22/less-than-half-of-u-s-kids-today-live-in-a-traditional-family/.

14.   Patrick Fagan and Robert Rector, *How Welfare Harms Kids,* The Heritage Foundation, June 5, 1996, http://www.heritage.org/research/reports/1996/06/bg1084nbsp-how-welfare-harms-kids.

9

1. Cathy LeBoeuf-Schouten, "My Canadian Healthcare Horror Stories: A Message for Americans," Lew Rockwell.com, August 11, 2009, https://www.lewrockwell.com/2009/08/cathy-leboeuf-schouten/my-canadian-healthcare-horror-stories/.

2. John C. Goodman, Gerald L. Musgrave, and Devon M. Herrick, *Lives at Risk: Single-Payer National Health Insurance Around the World* (Lanham: Rowman & Littlefield, 2004), 18.

3. Ibid., 19.

4. Ibid., 21.

5. "Health Care for All in Canada Did Not Include Laura Hillier," Dr.Hurd.com, February 9, 2016, https://drhurd.com/2016/02/09/57972/.

6. Ibid., 23.

7. Iris Winston, "Nursing Shortages a National Concern," canada.com, February 18, 2011, www.canada.com/health/Nursing+shortages+national+concern/4288871/story.html.

8. Carly Weeks, "Health Canada Warns of Worsening Drug Shortages," *Globe and Mail*, August 18, 2011, www.theglobeandmail.com/life/health-and-fitness/health-canada-warns-of-worsening-drug-shortages/article591014/.

9. "Ontario Hospital Bed Shortage Only to Get Worse: Ontario Health Coalition Report," Huffington Post, July 20, 2011, www.huffingtonpost.ca/2011/07/20/ontario-hospital-bed-shortage_n_905116.html.

10. "Hospitals Warn of Potential Medicine Shortage," CTV Montreal, February 28, 2014, http://montreal.

ctvnews.ca/hospitals-warn-of-potential-medicine-shortage-1.1709336.

11. Allison Cross, "Canadian Physician Shortage Will Take Time to Fix: Doctors," canada.com, August 4, 2010, www.canada.com/health/canadian+physician+shortage+will+take+time+doctors/2272360/story.html.

12. "Ontario Hospital Bed Shortage," www.huffingtonpost.ca/2011/07/20/ontario-hospital-bed-shorgage_n_905116.html.

13. James Brooke, "Full Hospitals Make Canadians Wait and Look South," *New York Times*, January 16, 2000, http://www.nytimes.com/2000/01/16/world/full-hospitals-make-canadians-wait-and-look-south.html.

14. Goodman, Musgrave, and Herrick, *Lives at Risk*, 28.

15. Ibid., 30.

16. Ibid., 32.

17. Ibid., 63.

18. "NHS Euthanasia Claims Ludicrous," BBC News, December 6, 1999, quoted in John C. Goodman, Gerald L. Musgrave, and Devon M. Herrick, *Lives at Risk: Single-Payer National Health Insurance Around the World* (Lanham: Rowman & Littlefield, 2004), 148.

19. Klaus Bernpaintner, "The Truth About Swedencare," Mises Daily, July 10, 2013, http://mises.org/library/truth-about-swedencare/.

20. Goodman, Musgrave, and Herrick, *Lives at Risk*, 11.

21. Yuri Maltsev, "What Soviet Medicine Teaches Us," Mises Daily, June 22, 2012, http://mises.org/library/what-soviet-medicine-teaches-us.
22. Ibid., 1.
23. Ibid., 3.
24. Ibid., 4.
25. Ibid.
26. Ibid.
27. Ibid.

10

1. Arthur C. Pigou, *Wealth and Welfare* (London: MacMillan, 1912).
2. Morton J. Horwitz, *The Transformation of American Law* (Cambridge: Harvard University Press, 1979).
3. See Terry L. Anderson and Donald R. Leal, eds., *Free Market Environmentalism for the Next Generation* (New York: Palgrave MacMillan, 2015).
4. Ibid.
5. Murray Reshbach, *Ecocide in the USSR* (New York: Basic Books, 1993).
6. The following is based on Thomas DiLorenzo, "How Socialism Causes Pollution," *The Freeman*, March 1, 1992, http://fee.org/articles/why-socialism-causes-pollution/.
7. Peter Gumbel, "Soviet Concerns About Pollution Danger Are Allowed to Emerge from the Closet," *Wall Street Journal*, August 23, 1988.
8. DiLorenzo, "Why Socialism Causes Pollution," 108.

9. Christine Lagorio, "The Most Polluted Places on Earth," CBS, June 6, 2007, http://www.cbsnews.com/news/the-most-polluted-places-on-earth/.

10. DiLorenzo, "Why Socialism Causes Pollution," 109.

11. Ibid.

12. Ibid.

13. Ibid., 110–111.

14. Corrosion Doctors, "Corrosion in Venezuela," http://corrosion-doctors.org/AtmCorros/mapVenezuela.htm.

15. Sylvie Lafont, "Pollution of Lake Maracaibo," Knowledge Base, August 29, 2012, http://www.akimoo.com/2012/pollution-of-lake-maracaibo/.

16. Jeroen Kuiper, "Venezuela's Environment Under Stress," venezuelanalysis.com, March 1, 2005, http://venezuelanalysis.com/analysis/973.

17. Ibid.

18. Ben Jervey, "Mexico's Pemex Plagued by Deadly Offshore Explosions and Major Pipeline Spills," DeSmog, May 26, 2015, http://www.desmogblog.com/2015/05/26/pemex-deadly-offshore-explosions-and-major-pipeline-spills.

19. Ibid.

20. Ibid.

21. "Flint Water Crisis Fast Facts," CNN, March 7, 2016, www.cnn.com/2016/03/04/us/flint-water-crisis-fast-facts/index.html.

11

1. John C. Calhoun, *A Disquisition on Government*, quoted in Ross Lence, ed., *Union and Liberty* (Indianapolis: Liberty Fund, 1992).
2. Ibid., 21.
3. Frank Chodorov, *The Income Tax: Root of All Evil* (Greenwich: Devin-Adair, 1954), 10.
4. Ibid., 11.
5. Ibid., 12.
6. Ibid.
7. Ibid., 13.
8. Ibid., 83.
9. Ibid.
10. Ibid., vii.
11. Ibid., vi.
12. Ludwig von Mises, *Omnipotent Government: The Rise of the Total State and Total War* (San Francisco: Libertarian Press, 1985), 268.
13. Felix Morley, *Freedom and Federalism* (Indianapolis: Liberty Fund, 1981), 3–4.
14. Adolf Hitler, *Mein Kampf* (New York: Houghton Mifflin, 1998), 565.
15. Ibid.
16. Ibid., 575.
17. Ibid., 578.
18. Gordon Tullock, *Welfare for the Well-to-Do* (London: Fisher Institute, 1983).
19. Timothy P. Carney, *The Big Ripoff: How Big Business and Big Government Steal Your Money* (New York: Wiley, 2006).

20. Robert Frank, "In Maryland, Higher Taxes Chase Out Rich: Study," CNBC, July 9, 2012, http://www.cnbc.com/id/48120446.

12

1. Greg Pason,"Socialists and the Living Wage Issue," The Socialist, February 19, 2015, http://www.thesocialist.us/socialists-and-the-living-wage-issue/.

2. Democratic Socialists of America, "The Minimum Wage: From Barely Tolerable to Basically Criminal," July 25, 2013, http://www.dsausa.org/the_minimum_wage.

3. Ibid., 2.

4. Ibid., 1.

5. J.R. Kearl et al., "What Economists Think," *American Economic Review* (May 1979): 30.

6. Paul Krugman and Robin Wells, *Microeconomics* (New York: Worth Publishing, 2015), 144.

7. Ibid.

8. Ibid.

9. Simon Rottenberg, "Minimum Wages in Puerto Rico," in *Economics of Legal Minimum Wages*, ed. Simon Rottenberg (Washington, DC: American Enterprise Institute, 1981), 330.

10. "Puerto Rico Hurt by Wage Hour Law," *New York Times*, October 24, 1938, 2.

11. Walter E. Williams, *Race and Economics* (Palo Alto: Hoover Institution Press, 2011), 42–43.

12. United States Department of Labor, "Employment Status of the Civilian Population by Race, Sex, and Age," www.bls.gov/news.release/empsit.t02.htm.
13. Walter E. Williams, "Government-Sanctioned Restraints That Reduce the Economic Opportunities for Minorities," *Policy Review* (Fall 1977):43.
14. Congressional Record, July 19, 1955, 10977.
15. Rottenberg, "Minimum Wages in Puerto Rico," 337.
16. Thomas Rustici, "A Public Choice View of the Minimum Wage," *Cato Journal* (Spring/Summer 1985):123.
17. Ibid., 124.
18. Ibid., 125.
19. Ibid.
20. Walter E. Williams, *Race and Economics*, 52.

13

1. Robert Heilbroner, "After Communism," *The New Yorker*, September 10, 1990, http://www.newyorker.com/magazine/1990/09/10/after-communism.
2. See George Stigler, *The Citizen and the State: Essays on Regulation* (Chicago: University of Chicago Press, 1975), 137.
3. Harold Demsetz, *Efficiency, Competition, and Policy* (Cambridge,: Blackwell, 1989), 78.
4. George T. Brown, *The Gas Light Company of Baltimore: A Study of Natural Monopoly* (Baltimore: Johns Hopkins University Press, 1936).
5. Ibid., 52.
6. Ibid., 75.

7. Ibid., 106.
8. Horace M. Gray, "The Passing of the Public Utility Concept," *Journal of Land and Public* Utility *Economics,* 16, no. 1 (February 1940): 9.
9. Ibid., 15.
10. Robert Higgs, *Crisis and Leviathan: Critical Episodes in the Growth of Government* (New York: Oxford University Press, 1987), 180.
11. Ibid.
12. Ibid., 179.
13. Ibid.
14. Ibid.
15. Meg Sullivan, "FDR Policies Prolonged Great Depression by 7 Years, UCLA Economists Calculate," UCLA Newsroom, August 10, 2004, http://newsroom.ucla.edu/releases/FDR-s-Policies-Prolonged-Depression-5409.
16. Alfred Kahn, "Airline Deregulation," The Concise Encyclopedia of Economics, http://www.econlib.org/library/Enc1/AirlineDeregulation.html.
17. Thomas Gale Moore, "Trucking Deregulation," The Concise Encyclopedia of Economics, http://www.econlib.org/library/Enc1/TruckingDeregulation.html.
18. Gabriel Kolko, *The Triumph of Conservatism* (New York: Free Press, 1977).
19. Dominick Armentano, *Antitrust and Monopoly* (New York: Wiley, 1982).

14

1. Karl Marx and Friedrich Engels, *Manifesto of the Communist Party* (New York: Cosimo Classics, 2009).

2. Robert Remini, *Andrew Jackson and the Bank War* (New York: Norton, 1967).

3. Murray N. Rothbard, *The Case Against the Fed* (Auburn: Ludwig von Mises Institute, 2007).

4. Murray N. Rothbard, *America's Great Depression* (Auburn: Ludwig von Mises Institute, 2000).

5. Bruno Frey, *Political Business Cycles* (London: Edward Elgar, 1997).

6. George Selgin, William Lastrapes, and Lawrence H. White, "Has the Fed Been a Failure?" (working paper, Cato Institute, Washington, DC, 2010), http://www.cato.org/publications/working-paper/has-fed-been-failure.

7. David Stockman, *The Great Deformation: The Corruption of Capitalism* (New York: Public Affairs Press, 2013).

8. Federal Reserve Board, *The Federal Reserve System: Purposes and Functions* (Washington, DC: Board of Governors of the Federal Reserve System, Washington, 2005), http://www.federalreserve.gov/pf/pf.htm.

9. "Government Agencies and Elected Officials," https://usa.gov/agencies.

10. See http://dodd-frank.com/.

11. Melissa C. Lott, "Solyndra-Illuminating Energy Funding Flaws?" *Scientific American*, September 27,

2011, http://blogs.scientificamerican.com/plugged-in/solyndra-illuminating-energy-funding-flaws/.

12. Matthew Mosk, "Obama Fundraisers Tied to Green Firms That Got Federal Cash," ABC News, September 29, 2011, http://abcnews.go.com/Blotter/obama-fundraisers-friends-green-firms-federal-cash/story?id=14592626.

15

1. "Per-Student Public School Spending in the U.S.," *Governing*, http://www.governing.com/gov-data/state-education-spending-per-pupil-data.html.
2. Ibid.
3. Dan Lips, Shanea Watkins, and John Fleming, "Does Spending More on Education Improve Academic Achievement?" *Backgrounder*, no. 2179 (September 8, 2008), http://thf_media.s3.amazon aws.com/2008/pdf/bg2179.pdf.
4. Ibid., 5.
5. Andrew Coulson, "State Education Trends: Academic Performance and Spending Over the Past 40 Years," *Policy Analysis* no. 746 (March 2014), http://object.cato.org/sites/cato.org/files/pubs/pdf/pa746.pdf.
6. Lips et al., "Does Spending More on Education Improve Academic Achievement?" 6.
7. Marx and Engels, *Manifesto of the Communist Party*.
8. "25-Point Program of the Nazi Party," http://www.historyplace.com/worldwar2/riseofhitler/25points.htm.

9.   Murray N. Rothbard, *Education: Free and Compulsory*, Mises Daily, September 9, 2006, http://mises.org/library/education-free-and-compulsory-0.
10. Ibid.
11. H.L. Mencken, *Prejudices: Third Series* (Ithaca: Cornell University Press, 2010).

16

1.   "Production for Use, Not for Profit" is labeled as one of the key principles of socialism on the website of the Socialist Party USA. See "Socialist Party USA," http://socialistparty-usa.net/principles.html.
2.   Ludwig von Mises, "Capitalism," Mises Daily, November 12, 2012, http://mises.org/library/capitalism.
3.   Burton Folsom, *The Myth of the Robber Barons* (Reston: Young America's Foundation, 1991).
4.   Ludwig von Mises, "The History of Capitalism," Mises Daily, July 30, 2010, https://mises.org/library/history-capitalism,1.
5.   Gary Walton and Hugh Rockoff, *History of the American Economy* (New York: Dryden Press, 1988), 242.
6.   Ibid., 408.
7.   Mises, "The History of Capitalism," 2.
8.   Michael Cox and Richard Alm, *Myths of Rich and Poor* (New York: Basic Books, 1993), 55.
9.   Ibid., 70-75.
10. Mises, "Capitalism,"5.

11. Burton Folsom, *Entrepreneurs vs. the State* (Herndon: Young America's Foundation, 1987), 2.
12. Thomas DiLorenzo, *How Capitalism Saved America* (New York: Three Rivers Press, 2004), 112.
13. Quoted in Albro Martin, *James J. Hill and the Opening of the Northwest* (New York: Oxford University Press, 1976), 411.
14. DiLorenzo, *How Capitalism Saved America*, 114.
15. Statement by Ida Tarbell, quoted in Dominick Armentano, *Antitrust and Monopoly* (New York: Wiley, 1982), 65.
16. Ibid., 59.
17. Thomas DiLorenzo, "The Myth of Predatory Pricing," *Cato Policy Analysis*, no. 169 (February 1992), http://www.cato.org/pubs/pas/pa-169.html.
18. John S. McGee, "Predatory Price Cutting: The Standard Oil (NJ) Case," *Journal of Law and Economics*, (October 1958):144–58.
19. Ludwig von Mises, *Omnipotent Government: The Rise of the Total State and Total War* (Indianapolis: Liberty Fund, 2011).

INDEX